SMOKING

Other Books in the At Issue Series:

SMOKING

David Bender, *Publisher*

Bruno Leone, *Executive Editor*

Katie de Koster, *Managing Editor*

Scott Barbour, *Series Editor*

Karin L. Swisher, *Book Editor*

An Opposing Viewpoints Series®

Greenhaven Press, Inc.
San Diego, California

Library of Congress Cataloging-in-Publication Data

At issue: smoking / book editor, Karin L. Swisher.
    p.   cm. — (At issue series) (An opposing viewpoints series)
    Includes bibliographical references and index.
    ISBN 1-56510-268-1 (pbk.) — ISBN 1-56510-301-7 (lib.).
    1. Tobacco habit—United States. 2. Tobacco—Physiological effects.
3. Smoking—Law and legislation—United States. [1. Smoking.]
I. Swisher, Karin, 1966-   . II. Title: Smoking. III. Series. IV. Series:
Opposing viewpoints series (Unnumbered)
HV5760.A86   1995   94-3600
362.29'6—dc20   CIP
                                                              AC

© 1995 by Greenhaven Press, Inc., PO Box 289009,
San Diego, CA 92198-9009

Printed in the U.S.A.

Every effort has been made to trace owners of copyrighted material.

Table of Contents

Introduction

In February 1994 David A. Kessler, commissioner of the Food and Drug Administration, testified before Congress that the FDA might decide to regulate nicotine as a drug. This declaration was one part of a current three-pronged attempt by the federal government to reduce smoking and the latest effort in a decades-long push to regulate tobacco. Since the surgeon general first declared smoking a health risk in 1964, many doctors and other public health experts have been involved in this antitobacco push. The tobacco industry, however, along with many smokers who believe their rights are being threatened, is actively opposing the antismoking drive.

Many private and governmental factions have opposed smoking as a health risk since the 1964 surgeon general's report on smoking and health linked smoking to cancer. Health experts, antismoking activists, and legislators have worked to pass a variety of regulations designed to reduce smoking. Many efforts have focused on the labeling of cigarette packages and on cigarette advertising. The first labeling law, the Cigarette Labeling and Advertising Act, took effect in 1966. It required cigarette packages and advertisements to warn that cigarette smoking "may be hazardous to your health." Another early legislative restriction was the 1969 Public Health Cigarette Smoking Act, which bans cigarette advertising on television and radio, leaving the tobacco industry only the print media and billboards on which to advertise. The Supreme Court upheld this ban one year later in the face of a challenge by the tobacco industry. The warning label was also strengthened to read, "Warning: The Surgeon General has determined that cigarette smoking is dangerous to your health." In 1984 the Comprehensive Smoking Education Act required the use of several different warning labels, which are rotated sequentially.

Government agencies also began to ban smoking in public spaces. In 1973, the Civil Aeronautics Board began requiring commercial airlines to offer nonsmoking sections. Later, smoking was banned on domestic flights of under two hours, and, in 1990, it was banned on all domestic flights of six hours or less. Also in 1973, the state of Arizona banned smoking in some public places. Other states followed suit, including Minnesota, which for many years had the most restrictive public smoking laws in the country. The Department of Health and Human Services in 1987 became the first federal agency to ban smoking in its offices. In 1993, the Environmental Protection Agency (EPA) released a report that linked environmental, or secondhand, tobacco smoke with cancer and other diseases among nonsmokers. The EPA report provided the necessary grounds for some congresspeople to propose a ban on smoking in all nonresidential buildings and also provided justification for other proposed regulations.

These past efforts provide a background for the current attack on smoking and tobacco by antismoking activists, health care experts, legislators, and government agencies. These partisans argue that smoking endangers health and thus costs the United States billions of dollars both in lost productivity and in health care treatment, and they contend that restricting smoking would significantly reduce these costs. The enemies of smoking are attacking it in three ways. First, they propose comprehensive, federal bans on smoking. Second, they propose tax increases on tobacco products. Finally, the FDA, for the first time, is considering regulating tobacco as a drug.

Many antismoking activists support regulatory measures such as the Smoke-Free Environment Act, initiated by Congressman Henry Waxman of California. The basis for this act was the EPA's 1993 report on environmental tobacco smoke. If passed, the act would outlaw smoking in virtually all nonresidential buildings. Supporters maintain that restrictions like those in the Smoke-Free Environment Act would reduce the health problems and other costs that result from environmental tobacco smoke. According to Waxman, the bill has a "simple, far-reaching goal: to protect the public from involuntary exposure to environmental tobacco smoke." The EPA contends that if the bill passes, the United States would save between $5 billion and $10 billion in building maintenance, between $6.5 billion and $19 billion in lost medical costs and productivity, and between 38,000 and 108,000 lives valued at $177 billion to $513 billion.

Another strategy favored by many antismoking activists is an increase in cigarette taxes. Currently federal and state taxes on cigarettes average 56 cents per pack. Proponents contend that if taxes were increased, many teenagers and lower-income smokers would be forced to cut down on the amount they smoke because they could not afford cigarettes at the higher price. Doctors Thomas D. MacKenzie, Carl E. Bartecchi, and Robert W. Schrier advocate such a tax in the *New England Journal of Medicine*. They write, "There are many potential benefits of increased tobacco taxes. First and most important, it is estimated that for every 10 percent increase in price, there will be a 4 percent reduction in tobacco consumption." Along with reducing tobacco consumption, advocates contend that increased taxes would also generate revenues to help cover the costs of health problems and lost productivity caused by smoking. According to Liberty Aldrich, a former program associate at the Advocacy Institute, a health and consumer advocacy organization in Washington, D.C., "Increasing tobacco taxes will cause a drop in consumption of cigarettes, promoting health and providing revenue to help cover the real costs of smoking." To this end, President Bill Clinton's 1993 health reform package included a proposed cigarette tax increase of 75 cents per pack.

A third strategy for reducing smoking is the potential FDA regulation of nicotine as a drug. The FDA can regulate a substance as a drug if its producer intends the product to "affect the structure or any function of the body." In his February 1994 testimony before Congress, FDA commissioner Kessler argued that the medical community has concluded that nicotine is addictive. He presented evidence indicating that cigarette manufacturers have long been aware of the addictive nature of nicotine, are able to manipulate nicotine levels in cigarettes, and may have done so to keep smokers addicted to their products. If so, according to Kessler, the actions of the tobacco industry constitute an intent to "affect the structure or any function of the body," and regulation of nicotine as a drug would be justified. If the FDA does eventually decide to regulate nicotine, one option would be to ban it as heroin and cocaine are banned. The FDA is more likely to recommend an incremental decrease in the nicotine level permitted in cigarettes until it reaches a level that would prevent addiction. Antismoking activists conclude that many smokers would then quit using cigarettes altogether.

These three strategies to reduce smoking have met with fierce resistance from several sources. In an effort to derail the federal government's push to reduce smoking, the tobacco industry and smokers' rights groups have been joined by organizations opposed to increasing government regulations. These various opponents reject the premise that the federal government should take responsibility for protecting smokers from any possible harms they may incur by smoking. They oppose most measures designed to reduce smoking.

Those who oppose bans on smoking argue that the alleged dangers of secondhand smoke are a false issue being exploited by politicians in their attack on smokers' individual rights. Many legislators, economists, and others argue that the EPA's conclusion that environmental tobacco smoke harms nonsmokers is erroneous. According to Jacob Sullum, a contributing editor of *Reason* magazine, "Even if exposure to ETS [environmental tobacco smoke] were analogous to smoking, the doses involved are so small that it's not clear they would have any effect." Critics maintain that the EPA's research is an example of the use of science for political purposes. Sullum writes, "The agency compromised science to support the political crusade against smoking." These opponents argue that rather than a legitimate attempt to protect public health, bans on smoking are an infringement on the individual rights of smokers. In the words of columnist Jeffery Hart, "Under our Constitution the federal government . . . has no jurisdiction whatever over the smoker."

Opponents of regulation also vehemently oppose any suggestion that cigarette taxes be increased. Many economists predict that while such a tax would in fact reduce the number of smokers, the financial disaster it would wreak on the tobacco industry in the rural South would counterbalance any economic benefits from reduced smoking. They predict that most tobacco growers—already fighting for shares of a decreasing market—would be forced out of business, especially since the land used for growing tobacco is suitable for little else. A representative of the Tobacco Growers Information Committee suggests, "Tobacco growers have to put up with so much attack, it seems to me if there were something else out there they could earn a living on, you can believe they would be looking into it." As one tobacco farmer in Sims, North Carolina, puts it, "A $1 increase in cigarette taxes would probably put half the tobacco farmers in this area out of business, and that's only a small minority of the people that would lose their jobs."

Along with this impact on tobacco growers, opponents charge, increased taxes would also lead to a cigarette black market. As evidence, many experts point to Canada's experience with high cigarette taxes. Between 1984 and 1992, federal and provincial governments in Canada raised taxes on tobacco by more than 200 percent. Canadian studies estimate that after the increase, one-sixth of the cigarettes consumed there were smuggled in and there is now a thriving black market on the streets. Some believe that the United States would have the same problem if tobacco taxes increased. According to one California tax administrator, "We've already noticed an increase in illegal activity in California as a result of our [state] tax increase."

The tobacco industry, led by such corporate giants as Philip Morris and RJ Reynolds, continues to fight smoking bans and cigarette tax increases, but the prospect of federal regulation of nicotine has led to even greater opposition. In response to FDA commissioner Kessler's testimony to Congress, the top executives of the nation's six largest tobacco companies appeared before Congress to argue that nicotine was not addictive and that nicotine levels in cigarettes were adjusted solely to enhance flavor. William I. Campbell, president and CEO of Philip Morris U.S.A., declared, "Our customers enjoy smoking for many reasons. Smokers are not drug addicts." The tobacco industry has also charged that cigarette regulations are merely the first step in a government campaign to regulate caffeine, high-fat foods, and other products that pose health risks.

The general trend in America is away from smoking. The tobacco companies, pushing hard to recruit new customers and keep the markets they have, see further regulation as a threat to the survival of the industry. Those in favor of increasing regulations to reduce smoking continue to press for smoking bans, higher taxes, and more stringent regulations. The battle is sure to continue. In *At Issue: Smoking*, various commentators express their opinions on cigarettes and smoking.

1

Smoking Should Be Regulated

Thomas D. MacKenzie, Carl E. Bartecchi, and Robert W. Schrier

Thomas D. MacKenzie, Carl E. Bartecchi, and Robert W. Schrier are members of the faculty of the department of medicine at the University of Colorado School of Medicine.

In terms of mortality, health, and lost wages, the costs of smoking to American society are astronomical. The tobacco industry, through advertising and lobbying, has succeeded in keeping those costs high, translating human suffering into profits both in the United States and around the world. The United States must curtail the tobacco industry's activities by banning all cigarette advertising, cutting government subsidies to tobacco farmers, restricting cigarette exports, increasing taxes on smoking, and banning all indoor smoking in public places.

The per capita consumption of cigarettes has risen and fallen, depending on particular events (Fig. 1)[1] Deaths from smoking-related illnesses, however, have climbed, possibly reaching a peak or plateau in 1988.[2] Studies[3] have placed the costs of smoking for the United States as a whole at a staggering $65 billion in 1985 in terms of health care expenditures and lost productivity, a value that would surely exceed $100 billion in current dollars. The estimated average lifetime medical costs for a smoker exceed those for a nonsmoker by more than $6,000.[4] This excess is a weighted average of costs incurred by all smokers, whether or not smoking-related illnesses develop. For smokers in whom such illnesses do develop, the personal financial impact is much higher.[4] The economic effect of smoking has not been overlooked by the life insurance companies. *Time* magazine reported[5] that even three insurance firms owned by tobacco companies charge smokers nearly double for term life insurance, because smokers are about twice as likely as nonsmokers to die at a given age.

The Congressional Office of Technology Assessment estimated in its 1993 report[6] that the total financial cost of smoking to society in 1990 was $2.59 per pack of cigarettes. Some experts argue that this cost is actually much higher. One study,[7] however, suggested that smokers may

Thomas D. MacKenzie, Carl E. Bartecchi, and Robert W. Schrier, "The Human Costs of Tobacco Use," part 2, *The New England Journal of Medicine*, vol. 330, no. 14 (April 7, 1994), pp. 975-80. Reprinted by permission.

pay their own way at the current level of excise taxes mostly because they do not live long enough to enjoy their share of the Social Security and pension benefits for which they have paid. This conclusion is controversial; moreover, most would agree that premature deaths due to smoking are not a humane means of controlling health care costs.

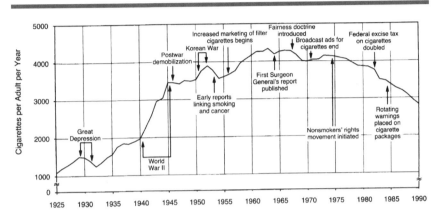

Figure 1. Per Capita Consumption of Cigarettes among Adults in the United States from 1925 to 1990, in Relation to Certain Historical Events.

Data were obtained from the Department of Health and Human Services.[1]

Another economic consideration is the cost associated with employees who smoke. Cigarette smokers are absent from work approximately 6.5 days more per year than nonsmokers. They make about six visits more to health care facilities per year than nonsmokers, and dependents of smokers make about four visits more per year than nonsmokers.[8] The cost to employers of workers who smoke is considerable and reflects costs due to work absences, health care claims, benefits not related to health care, and decreased productivity.[9] The Office of Technology Assessment[6] estimates the costs of lost productivity of persons disabled by diseases attributable to smoking and forfeited earnings of those dying prematurely of such diseases at $47 billion for 1990. With the use of 1985 figures, the costs of lost productivity due to passive smoking were estimated to be $8.6 billion annually.[10]

Fires related to cigarette smoking are the leading cause of civilian fire deaths in the United States. In 1983, the U.S. Fire Administration estimated that fires caused by cigarettes killed more than 2300 men, women, and children and burned more than 5000 others in the United States.[11] The health care costs related to the care of burn victims from such fires are also substantial. The most recent data (1991) from the National Fire Protection Association (unpublished data) list 187,100 fires caused by smoking materials, which caused an estimated $552 million in direct property damage.

The tobacco industry

Despite a 20-year trend of declining tobacco consumption in the United States, tobacco sales remain highly profitable. The U.S. tobacco industry is led by Philip Morris and RJR Nabisco, which together controlled 70 percent of the U.S. market in 1988.[12] In 1992, Philip Morris was the seventh largest industrial corporation in the United States, with $50 billion in sales. When these corporations were ranked according to profits, however, Philip Morris made more money in 1992—$4.9 billion—than any other company in the United States, reflecting the large profit margin of cigarette sales.[13] This economic success in the face of declining U.S. cigarette consumption involved pricing that more than compensated for both inflation and the decrease in domestic sales. Aggressive advertising and marketing, as well as expanding exportation of tobacco, were also important factors.

Tobacco advertising and marketing

Cigarette advertising and promotion, despite some government restrictions, have undergone unbridled expansion in the past 30 years. Three years after the publication of the 1964 Surgeon General's report on the ill effects of smoking, the Federal Communications Commission, according to the Fairness Doctrine, ruled that local television and radio stations that broadcast cigarette advertising must also broadcast a balance of tobacco counteradvertising. Cigarette consumption per capita subsequently declined (Fig. 1)[1, 14] With the Public Health Cigarette Smoking Act of 1969, Congress banned all cigarette advertising on electronic media.[15] The outcome of this regulation has been the subject of great discussion. Advertising against smoking in the electronic media ceased, and cigarette advertising in magazines and newspapers and on billboards increased dramatically.[16] Warner and Goldenhar have reported in a study of 39 magazines that carried cigarette advertisements before and after the electronic-media ban was enforced in 1971 that advertising revenue from the tobacco industry increased by $5.5 million per magazine per year in constant 1983 dollars.[17] Moreover, the coverage of smoking and health issues decreased by 65 percent in magazines that carried cigarette advertisements, as compared with a decrease of 29 percent in magazines that did not.[17] For three years after the ban, per capita tobacco consumption in the United States, which had been declining before the ban, actually increased (Fig. 1).[1]

Most would agree that premature deaths due to smoking are not a humane means of controlling health care costs.

Since the electronic-media ban, advertising expenditures by the tobacco industry have risen dramatically. From 1975 to 1990, annual expenditures on cigarette advertising and promotional events grew from $500 million to $3.9 billion. In constant 1975 dollars this represents more than a threefold increase.[18, 16] In 1989, Philip Morris had the largest advertising budget of any company in the United States, spending $2 billion to promote its products.[19] In 1988, cigarettes were the most advertised prod-

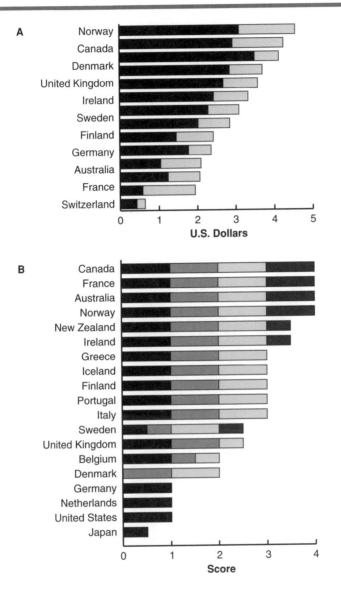

Figure 2. Average Retail Price of a Pack of 20 Cigarettes in Various Countries in 1993 (Panel A) and Regulations Governing Cigarette Advertising in Industrialized Nations (Panel B).

In Panel A, the average total tax per pack is shown in ■. The total tax as a percentage of the retail price is given to the right of each bar (Non-smokers Rights Association of Canada: unpublished data). In Panel B, countries were accorded 1 point for a ban and ½ point for restrictions on electronic (■), print (■), and billboard (▩) tobacco advertisements and event sponsorship (■). Data were adapted from Samuels et al.[30]

uct on billboards and the second most advertised product in print media.[16] Promotional expenditures, which include the sponsorship of sporting events and the distribution of free cigarettes and coupons, have grown from one quarter of the marketing budget in 1975 to two thirds in 1988.[16]

A large portion of the marketing budget allocated for promotion supports sponsorship of events such as the Virginia Slims tennis tournament, the Marlboro Grand Prix, and Camel Motocross. The appeal of motor racing to the tobacco industry is not surprising, since it ranks as the second largest spectator sport in the United States behind football.[15] The economics of this high visibility are not lost on RJR Nabisco, which has become the leading sponsor of automobile and motorcycle racing in the United States. Far more important than the audience attending any such event, however, is the audience watching the event on television. For example, during the 93-minute broadcast of the 1989 Marlboro Grand Prix, the Marlboro name was mentioned 11 times and the logo was shown 5922 times, for a total of 46 minutes of exposure. Eighteen minutes of this exposure consisted of "clear, in-focus air time" estimated to have a commercial value of over $1 million.[15]

At what audience are the advertising and promotion by tobacco companies aimed? Recent data on the Camel-cigarette advertising campaign suggest that a principal target group is children. In 1988, with Camel sales declining, RJR Nabisco launched a marketing campaign featuring Old Joe Camel, a "smooth character" presumably modeled after James Bond.[20] In the advertisements, Old Joe rides motorcycles, shoots pool, and associates with attractive women while smoking Camel cigarettes. Three years into the campaign, Pierce et al. showed that 14 percent of adults over the age of 18 identified Camel as the most advertised cigarette brand, whereas 29 percent of teenagers 12 to 17 years of age and 34 percent of 12- to 13-year-olds believed Camel was the most advertised brand.[21] Even more striking are the data from Fischer et al. showing that 30 percent of 3-year-olds and over 80 percent of 6-year-olds are able to associate a picture of Old Joe Camel with a pack of cigarettes. Among 6-year-olds, the same percentage associated a package of cigarettes with Old Joe Camel as were able to associate a picture of the Disney Channel logo with Mickey Mouse.[22] Other evidence suggesting that children are a target market for cigarettes is RJR Nabisco's sponsorship of events such as the "Camel Mud and Monster Series," tobacco-company–sponsored promotion of brand-name cigarettes in movies aimed at teenage audiences,[23] and the appearance of cigarette advertisements in teen magazines. Currently, a pack of Camel cigarettes comes with a "C-note" that can be used to purchase Camel products with great appeal to teenagers, such as Camel charm earrings, a tropical shower curtain, or a watch with Old Joe Camel on the face.

Since the electronic-media ban, advertising expenditures by the tobacco industry have risen dramatically.

From a marketing standpoint, the Camel campaign has been very successful. DiFranza et al.[20] compared brand preference in 1988 and 1990 and reported that the proportion of smokers under the age of 18 who smoked Camels had increased from 0.5 percent to 32 percent since the start of the Old Joe campaign. These authors estimated that sales of

Camel cigarettes to smokers under the age of 18 had increased from $6 million to $476 million, accounting for one quarter of all Camel sales and one third of all illegal sales of cigarettes.[20]

Since 1992, the decline in per capita cigarette consumption, which had been uninterrupted since 1973, has ended.[18] This dramatic change has occurred simultaneously with the rapid growth of generic brands and low-priced brand-name cigarettes, which now control 36 percent of the market share.[24] This trend has decreased the average price of cigarettes and forced a landmark price cut in the spring of 1993, first by Philip Morris (Marlboro) and subsequently by its leading competitors. These events may have a lasting impact not only on industry profits but also on smoking prevalence rates, especially among populations that are sensitive to changes in prices, such as teenagers.

Tobacco exportation

The U.S. tobacco industry, which is second only to China in tobacco production, has recently expanded its activity in foreign markets. Cigarette exportation has increased dramatically since 1984 and has offset declining consumption in the United States such that domestic cigarette production has been maintained.[25] In 1984, the United States exported 56 billion cigarettes, or 8 percent of its total production. In 1991, however, the United States exported 194 billion cigarettes, which accounted for over 25 percent of total production. The United States exports more than three times as many cigarettes as does any other country in the world.[26]

In some developing countries, little emphasis is placed on the hazards of smoking, and hence there is no legislation governing warning labels, advertising restrictions, or tar content. This has provided the powerful transnational tobacco companies with an opportunity to penetrate foreign markets rapidly. The U.S. government has not thwarted this expansion, and there are several possible reasons for its inaction. First of all, the United States realized a $3.5 billion trade surplus from tobacco exports in 1988, up from $2.5 billion in 1987.[27] The effect of this surplus on the trade deficit may have foiled any political efforts to limit the exportation or regulate the packaging (i.e., warning labels) of tobacco products. Furthermore, U.S. trade representatives, at the request of the tobacco industry (under section 301 of the 1974 Trade Act), have pressured foreign governments to open their markets to the transnational tobacco companies and to lift restrictions on cigarette advertising on television and in print.[27] Some have asked whether it is any less morally offensive for the United States to export cigarettes in the 1990s to lessen the trade deficit than it was for England to export opium to China in the 1830s to balance imports of silk and tea.[28]

With respect to the exportation of tobacco, Dr. James Mason, former assistant secretary for health in the Department of Health and Human Services, was quoted as saying:

> Cigarettes become a health problem only when you combine addiction with greed—greed on the part of the tobacco industry and the advertising industry, who are willing to exchange dollars for the lives of others. Our country has been known for its humanitarian and health-related projects worldwide. This is a hundred and eighty degrees opposite. We're talking about millions of lives—and that totally outweighs and overwhelms what we've accomplished in the humanitarian field. It's outrageous for the United States to allow this misery and suffering to occur.[29]

Cigarettes remain the only consumer product sold legally in the United States that is unequivocally carcinogenic when used as directed. Despite mountains of evidence on the health hazards of smoking cigarettes, the American public and government have tolerated the relatively unregulated advertisement, promotion, and sale of such a product. This passive tolerance is fueled in part by one of the most powerful political lobbies in government.

Cigarettes become a health problem only when you combine addiction with greed—greed on the part of the tobacco industry and the advertising industry.

During the 1992 presidential campaign, the tobacco industry gave $2.5 million to the political parties, which represents a fivefold increase in funds contributed in 1988. In addition, contributions to House and Senate candidates during the 1992 campaign by tobacco political action committees exceeded $2.2 million, nearly twice the amount contributed from 1989 through 1990[30, 31] (and Samuels B, et al.: personal communication).

Working at the level of the local, state, and federal governments, tobacco-company lobbyists are described by Representative Mike Synar (D-Okla.) as "the most pervasive group in politics today."[31] Their activities include the formation and financial support of so-called grass-roots smokers' rights groups and local business coalitions designed to fight local tobacco-control legislation.[32] The Tobacco Institute and the Council for Tobacco Research, which are funded by the tobacco industry, ostensibly support the study of questions about tobacco use and health and "remain committed to advancing scientific inquiry into the gaps of knowledge in the smoking controversy."[33] As late as 1986, however, a Tobacco Institute publication stated that "eminent scientists believe that questions relating to smoking and health are unresolved."[33] These statements raise doubt in the minds of the public and their government representatives over a scientific debate that has been settled for nearly 30 years—namely, that cigarettes cause lethal disease in humans.

The campaign to prevent tobacco use

Although cigarette smoking is the number-one preventable cause of premature death in our society, nearly 50 million Americans still smoke. There are several reasons for this tragic situation. First, the American public is reluctant to change a habit that is both culturally ingrained in their society and powerfully addictive, perhaps as addictive as the use of heroin and cocaine.[34] Second, recognition of the magnitude of this health hazard by U.S. citizens and their government has been hindered by the tobacco industry's expenditure of $4 billion per year for advertising and promotion. Third, the efforts of the tobacco industry to fight legislation on tobacco taxes have resulted in a lower excise tax on tobacco products, as a percentage of the retail price, in this country than in any of the other industrialized nations listed in Figure 2A (Non-smokers Rights Association of Canada: unpublished data); the United States also has among the least restrictive advertising regulations in the industrialized world (Fig. 2B).[30] Furthermore, tobacco products are not subject to regulation by the Food and Drug Administration[35] or by the Consumer Product Safety Commission,[36] which would, given current standards of product safety, undeniably prevent the sale of a similar product were it introduced today. Thus, the obstacles facing the campaign against tobacco use are formidable. To be effective, this campaign must operate on many different levels, from community education programs to support for increases in federal excise taxes (Table 1).

Smoking restrictions in the workplace and in public

Over the past 10 years, public recognition of the dangers of passive smoking (i.e., environmental tobacco smoke) has steadily increased. From 1980 to 1989, the number of no-smoking laws passed by various cities increased 10-fold, and by 1989, 44 states had passed some form of smoking-control legislation.[37] There is great variability, however, among no-smoking laws. Among 902 cities and all 50 states surveyed in a recent study, only 17 percent of the cities and 20 percent of the states had comprehensive laws restricting smoking in government buildings, public places, restaurants, and private workplaces.[37] Nevertheless, it has been shown that local efforts to initiate tobacco-control legislation as a means of protecting citizens against the ill effects of environmental tobacco smoke can overcome tobacco-industry efforts if supported by a strong coalition of community members, local businesses, and sympathetic political leadership.[32]

Bans on advertising

As discussed, cigarettes remain the second most heavily advertised product in the United States, behind automobiles.[38] The American Medical Association is among the many institutions that have recommended a ban on all cigarette advertisements and promotional activities. Several bills have been proposed in Congress either to restrict further cigarette advertising or to ban it totally, though none have passed.[39] A strong tobacco lobby has argued that a ban on advertising would violate the industry's constitutional rights of free expression. A close examination of modern case law and the Supreme Court interpretation of the commercial free-speech doctrine, however, reveals that there are precedents for imposing restrictions on the advertisement of legal products when consumer safety is threatened.[35]

Restrictions on sales of tobacco to minors

Approximately 80 to 90 percent of regular smokers start smoking by the age of 18. To influence smoking-related public health outcomes, efforts must be made to limit the availability of cigarettes to minors. An increasing number of states have appropriately supported such legislation. Currently, 46 states have laws prohibiting the sale of tobacco products to minors.[40] Compliance with these laws, however, has been repeatedly shown to be poor.[41-44] Attempts by minors to purchase cigarettes in eight communities in four separate studies had a success rate of 46 to 88 percent. Furthermore, only 22 states have laws prohibiting the free distribution of tobacco products to minors, and only 9 states ban the sale of tobacco products in vending machines or restrict the placement of such vending machines.[40] These data suggest that our society is remarkably passive about the illegal sale of addictive and dangerous tobacco products to children.

On the one hand, the Department of Health and Human Services discourages tobacco use among U.S. citizens, whereas on the other hand the Department of Agriculture uses taxpayers' dollars to subsidize the tobacco industry,[45] and the Internal Revenue Service allows the tobacco industry to deduct 100 percent of its advertising and promotional expenditures.[46] Although this tax deduction is not unique to the tobacco industry, given the health consequences of the product and the focus of the advertisements on women, children, and minorities, the U.S. public should be outraged by the mixed messages from our government. Substantial government subsidies to allow conversion from tobacco to other profitable and needed crops would seem indicated.

Table 1.   Essential Components of a Campaign to Prevent Tobacco Use.

- Increased federal excise taxes
- Comprehensive restrictions on smoking in the workplace and in public
- Bans on advertising and sponsorship by tobacco companies
- Comprehensive and enforced restrictions on sales of tobacco to minors
- Limitation of tobacco-crop subsidies
- Government support for conversion of tobacco crops to other crops
- Financial support for tobacco counteradvertising
- Enhanced community-education programs
- Divestment of tobacco-company stocks by universities and public institutions
- Support for personal-injury litigation against the tobacco industry
- Physician-supervised counseling on smoking cessation

The federal excise tax on cigarettes has increased from 8 cents per pack in 1951 to the current 24 cents per pack.[47] With the addition of state cigarette taxes, the average total tax on a pack of cigarettes in the United States is 56 cents, or approximately 30 percent of the retail price. This percentage is dramatically lower than that in all the other industrialized countries listed in Figure 2A (Non-smokers Rights Association of Canada: unpublished data). Switzerland, which taxes cigarettes at 50 percent of the retail price, has the next lowest tax. An increase in the federal tobacco tax of $2 per pack of cigarettes has been recommended by the American Heart Association, the American Lung Association, and the American Cancer Society. Such an increase would still place the United States behind many countries (Fig. 2A). In March 1993, Senator Bill Bradley (D-N.J.) and Representative Mike Andrews (D-Tex.) introduced the Tobacco Health Tax Act of 1993, which would raise the federal excise tax to $1 per pack of cigarettes. Unfortunately, the Clinton Health Care Security Act proposes an increase of only 75 cents per pack.

There are many potential benefits of increased tobacco taxes. First and most important, it is estimated that for every 10 percent increase in price, there will be a 4 percent reduction in tobacco consumption.[1] This figure is likely to be even higher in populations, such as teenagers, that are most sensitive to changes in prices. The effect of user fees has been clearly demonstrated by the small (25 cent) increase in the state cigarette tax in California approved in 1989, which resulted in a substantial acceleration in the decline of tobacco consumption as compared with the rates of decline in the rest of the United States.[48] Similarly, Canada increased federal and provincial cigarette taxes from an average of 46 cents in 1980 to $3.72 in 1991. During this time, cigarette sales fell 39 percent,[49] tobacco consumption decreased 30 percent faster than in the United States,[50] and smoking by teenagers was cut by two thirds.[47] With the recent fall in the prices of Marlboro, Camel, and other brand-name cigarettes, an increase in the cigarette tax becomes particularly important to counteract a potential increase in consumption among teenagers.

Efforts must be made to limit the availability of cigarettes to minors.

Second, with an increase in the cigarette tax, the resultant decline in consumption will lead to a decline in health care costs as former smokers and their children require less medical care. Third, since the Health Security Act estimates that $105 billion in revenues will be generated over a five-year period by a 75-cent increase in the tax on a pack of cigarettes, a $2 increase could yield as much as $250 billion over the same period. This not only would allow the tobacco industry to pay more equitably for the excess economic burden placed by its products on the health care system, but also could provide important funds for universal access to health care. Revenue generated by an increase in the tobacco tax could also be used to pay for community education and advertising against tobacco. Opponents of the increase in the tobacco tax argue that it is a regressive tax, like that on gasoline or food. Cigarettes are, however, lethal consumer products and cannot be considered in the same class as gasoline and food.

Tobacco use has exacted a tragic toll on the U.S population. Every segment of our society suffers the consequences of these addictive products, including disproportionate effects on children, women, and minorities. The human and economic costs of tobacco use to our society are overwhelming. A uniform ban on tobacco advertisements, an increase in the number of laws against smoking in public places, more aggressive public education, and a higher tax on cigarettes would diminish some of the human tragedies of tobacco use.

Notes:

1. Strategies to control tobacco use in the United States: a blueprint for public health action in the 1990's. Smoking and tobacco control monographs no. 1. Rockville, Md.: Department of Health and Human Services, 1991. (NIH publication no. 92-3316.)

2. Cigarette smoking-attributable mortality and years of potential life lost—United States, 1990. MMWR Morb Mortal Wkly Rep 1993; 42:645-9.

3. Schelling TC. Economics and cigarettes. Prev Med 1986; 15:549-60.

4. Smoking and health in the Americas: a 1992 report of the Surgeon Gen-

eral, in collaboration with the Pan American Health Organization: executive summary. Atlanta: Department of Health and Human Services, 1992. (DHHS publication no. (CDC) 92-8421.)

5. Tobias A. The dividends for quitters. Time. October 12, 1992:76.

6. Smoking-related deaths and financial costs: estimates for 1990. Rev. ed. Washington, D.C.: Office of Technology assessment, 1993.

7. Manning WG, Keeler EB, Newhouse JP, Sloss EM, Wasserman J. The taxes of sin: do smokers and drinkers pay their way? JAMA 1989; 261:1604-9.

8. Lesmes GR. Corporate healthcare costs and smoke-free environments. Am J Med 1992; 93:Suppl 1A:1A-48S-1A-54S.

9. Bertera RL. The effects of behavioral risks on absenteeism and health-care costs in the workplace. J Occup Med 1991; 33:1119-24.

10. Lesmes GR, Donofrio KH. Passive smoking: the medical and economic issues. Am J Med 1992; 93:Suppl 1A:1A-38S-1A-42S.

11. McGuire A. Cigarettes and fire deaths. N Y State J Med 1983;83:1296-8.

12. Elliot S. Tobacco firms match challenges. USA Today. May 24, 1988:1 B-2B.

13. Faltermayer E. The Fortune 500: poised for a comeback. Fortune. April 19, 1993:174-240.

14. Garfinkel L, Silverberg E. Lung cancer and smoking trends in the United States over the past 25 years. CA Cancer J Clin 1991;41:137-45.

15. Blum A. The Marlboro Grand Prix: circumvention of the television ban on tobacco advertising. N Engl J Med 1991;324:913-7.

16. Cigarette advertising—United States, 1988. MMWR Morb Mortal Wkly Rep 1990;39:261-5.

17. Warner KE, Goldenhar LM. The cigarette advertising broadcast ban and magazine coverage of smoking and health. J Public Health Policy 1989;10:32-42.

18. Cigarette smoking among adults—United States, 1991. MMWR Morb Mortal Wkly Rep 1993; 42:230-3.

19. From chuck wagon to trail boss of Marlboro country. Business Week. April 15, 1991:60-5.

20. DiFranza JR, Richards JW, Paulman PM, et al. RJR Nabisco's cartoon camel promotes Camel cigarettes to children. JAMA 1991;266:314953.

21. Pierce JP, Gilpin E, Burns DM, et al. Does tobacco advertising target young people to start smoking? Evidence from California. JAMA 1991;266:3154-8.

22. Fischer PM, Schwartz MP, Richards JW Jr, Goldstein AO, Rojas TH. Brand logo recognition by children aged 3 to 6 years: Mickey Mouse and Old Joe the Camel. JAMA 1991;266:3145-8.

23. Cigarette ads in kids' movies. Tob Youth Rep 1989;4:1.

24. Cigarette burn: price cut on Marlboro upsets rosy notions about tobacco profits. Wall Street Journal. April 5, 1993:A1, A7.

25. Situation and outlook report: tobacco. Washington, D.C.: Department of Agriculture, Economic Research Service, 1992. (Report TS-220.)

26. World tobacco situation. Washington, D.C.: Department of Agriculture, Foreign Agricultural Service, 1992. (Document FT-8-92.)

27. Connolly GN. Worldwide expansion of transnational tobacco industry. Monogr Natl Cancer Inst 1992;12:29-35.

28. Mintz M. Tobacco roads: delivering death to the third world. The Progressive. May 1991:24-9.

29. Sesser S. Opium war redux. The New Yorker. September 13, 1993:78-89.

30. Samuels B, Douglass C, Wolfe S, Wilbur P. Tobacco money, tobacco people, tobacco policies. Advocacy Institute Report. August 1992.

31. Morrissey M. Tobacco turns over a new (green) leaf. Natl J 1992;September 12:2073-5.

32. Samuels B, Glantz SA. The politics of local tobacco control. JAMA 1991;266:2110-7.

33. Warner KE. Tobacco industry scientific advisors: serving society or selling cigarettes? Am J Public Health 1991;81:839-42.

34. The health consequences of smoking: nicotine addiction: a report of the Surgeon General. Rockville, Md.: Department of Health and Human Services, 1988:15. (DHHS publication no. (CDC) 88-8406.)

35. Gostin LO, Brandt AM. Criteria for evaluating a ban on the advertisement of cigarettes: balancing public health benefits with constitutional burdens. JAMA 1993;269:904-9.

36. Consumer Product Safety Act, 15 U.S.C., §2051.

37. Rigotti NA, Pashos CL. No-smoking laws in the United States: an analysis of state and city actions to limit smoking in public places and workplaces. JAMA 1991;266:3162-7.

38. The health consequences of involuntary smoking: a report of the Surgeon General. Rockville, Md.: Department of Health and Human Services, 1986. (DHHS publication no. (CDC) 87-8398.)

39. Rovner J. House subcommittee approves strong antitobacco measure. Congr Q 1990;September 15:2922-3.

40. State tobacco prevention and control activities: results of the 1989-1990 Association of State and Territorial Health Officials (ASTHO) survey final report. MMWR Morb Mortal Wkly Rep 1991;40(RR-11):1-41.

41. Minors' access to tobacco—Missouri, 1992, and Texas, 1993. MMWR Morb Mortal Wkly Rep 1993;42:125-8.

42. Jason LA, Ji PY, Anes MD, Birkhead SH. Active enforcement of cigarette control laws in the prevention of cigarette sales to minors. JAMA 1991;266:3159-61.

43. Feighery E, Altman DG, Shaffer G. The effects of combining education and enforcement to reduce tobacco sales to minors: a study of four northern California communities. JAMA 1991;266:3168-71.

44. DiFranza JR, Brown LJ. The Tobacco Institute's "It's the Law" campaign: has it halted illegal sales of tobacco to children? Am J Public Health 1992;82:1271-3.

45. Warner KE. The tobacco subsidy: does it matter? J Natl Cancer Inst 1988;80:81-3.

46. Harkin T. Cut the taxpayers' subsidy of cigarette advertising. Christian Science Monitor. October 13, 1992:19.

47. Novak V. Kicking the habit. Natl J 1993;April 17:912-6.

48. Flewelling RL, Kenney E, Elder JP, Pierce J, Johnson M, Bal DG. First-year impact of the 1989 California cigarette tax increase on cigarette consumption. Am J Public Health 1992;82:867-9.

49. Kaiserman MJ, Rogers B. Forty year trends in Canadian tobacco sales. Can J Public Health 1992;83:404-6.

50. *Idem*. Tobacco consumption declining faster in Canada than in the US. Am J Public Health 1991;81:902-4.

2

Smoking Should Be Banned in Nonresidential Buildings

Henry A. Waxman

Henry A. Waxman, a Democratic representative from California, chairs the Health and the Environment Subcommittee of the House Energy and Commerce Committee.

The health risks of environmental tobacco smoke (ETS) concern many Americans. In order to reduce the health hazards posed by ETS, Congress should ban smoking in all nonresidential buildings.

Congress has the chance to pass a law that would save more than 38,000 American lives each year. This law would cost virtually nothing to implement; in fact, it would actually save the economy billions each year.

The law is the Smoke-Free Environment Act, and it has a simple, but far-reaching goal: to protect the public from involuntary exposure to environmental tobacco smoke.

If enacted, it would require the adoption of smoke-free policies in virtually all nonresidential buildings.

The Smoke-Free Environment Act may sound audacious to some, but when the facts are considered, it's just plain common sense.

A known carcinogen

Environmental tobacco smoke—the secondhand cigarette smoke breathed by nonsmokers—is a known human carcinogen and the most dangerous environmental pollutant most Americans face. According to the American Medical Association, it is the third leading cause of premature death in the United States, killing more than 50,000 Americans each year through heart disease and cancer.

Incredible as it may seem, more people die each year as a result of breathing someone else's cigarette smoke than die in motor vehicle accidents.

Our children suffer the most from environmental tobacco smoke. Each year, exposure to tobacco smoke causes 150,000 to 300,000 cases of bronchitis and pneumonia in infants and young children. As many as a

Henry A. Waxman, "Ban Indoor Smoking . . . Everywhere but Home?" *The Washington Times,* February 13, 1994. Reprinted by permission of the author.

million children suffer asthma attacks when exposed to the smoke of even a single cigarette.

The benefits of going smoke-free are enormous—and not only to nonsmokers. Smokers gain too, because quitting becomes much easier, and millions of youths will never start smoking if there's no place to light up. The costs of building maintenance also will drop significantly.

According to the Environmental Protection Agency, compliance with the Smoke-Free Environment Act would cost less than $1 billion each year. For this investment, each year the nation would save hundreds of billions of dollars, including: (1) $5 billion to $10 billion in the costs of building maintenance; (2) $6.5 billion to $19 billion in avoided medical costs and increased productivity; and (3) 38,000 to 108,000 lives, valued conservatively at $177 billion to $513 billion.

Truly, this is an opportunity we cannot afford to miss.

In an unprecedented joint appearance before Congress, the current and five former surgeons general—representing four Republican and two Democratic administrations—called the Smoke-Free Environment Act the most important public health measure to come before Congress in years.

Environmental tobacco smoke . . . is a known human carcinogen and the most dangerous environmental pollutant most Americans face.

Of course, the tobacco industry doesn't see things this way. The industry, which still denies even that active smoking kills, argues that exposure to carcinogenic environmental tobacco smoke is harmless. Hyperventilated tobacco lobbyists condemn the Smoke-Free Environment Act as "social engineering on a vast scale . . . recalling the extremism of Prohibition."

The analogy to Prohibition is wrong; the right analogy is drunk driving. Our laws don't ban drinking, but they do outlaw drinking while you drive because of the risks to others.

Similarly, the Smoke-Free Environment Act doesn't ban smoking, but only smoking in places where the health of others is jeopardized. Indeed, the bill specifically allows companies to set up separately ventilated smoking lounges, where smokers could smoke without endangering others.

The American public has awakened to the dangers of environmental tobacco smoke and is demanding tough federal action. So, too, has the business community. The Building Owners and Managers Association, which represents the commercial real estate industry, supports a federal ban on smoking indoors.

The choice really comes down to our children vs. the tobacco companies. Members of Congress must decide whether to listen to the well-heeled tobacco lobby or to what doctors say is necessary to protect kids' health.

The Clinton administration came down in favor of kids and endorsed the Smoke-Free Environment Act. The rest is up to Congress.

If, like me, you feel strongly about this issue, make sure you contact your elected representatives. Together, we can defeat the tobacco industry and guarantee each of us a healthy and smoke-free environment.

3

Regulations on Smoking Reduce the Dangers of Secondhand Smoke

Carol M. Browner

Carol M. Browner is the administrator of the Environmental Protection Agency.

The Environmental Protection Agency (EPA) has concluded that environmental tobacco smoke is a human carcinogen and is responsible for approximately 3,000 deaths every year. The EPA recommends regulations prohibiting smoking along with public policies that reduce exposure to secondhand smoke.

Environmental tobacco smoke (ETS), also termed secondhand smoke, harms the health of thousands of Americans each year. ETS is a mixture of the smoke given off by the burning end of cigarettes, pipes, or cigars, and the smoke exhaled from the lungs of smokers. This mixture contains over 4,000 substances. More than 40 of these are known to cause cancer in humans and animals, and many are strong respiratory irritants.

Exposure to secondhand smoke, called involuntary smoking or passive smoking, is concentrated indoors, where ETS is often the most significant pollutant. Indoor levels of the particles you may inhale (the "tars" in the cigarettes) from ETS often exceed the national air quality standard established by EPA [Environmental Protection Agency] for outdoor air. The high levels of carbon monoxide in secondhand smoke also warrant concern.

In January 1993, EPA released an assessment of the health risks of passive smoking in a report entitled *Respiratory Health Effects of Passive Smoking: Lung Cancer and Other Disorders*. The report summarizes the findings of an extensive investigation conducted by the Agency. It incorporates comments from two open public reviews and recommendations from EPA's Science Advisory Board—a panel of independent scientific experts in this field. The board endorsed the conclusions of the report and the methodologies used. In particular, the board unanimously endorsed the report's classification of ETS as a human lung carcinogen.

Carol M. Browner, "Environmental Tobacco Smoke: EPA's Report," *EPA Journal*, October/December 1993.

Based on the overall weight of available scientific evidence, EPA concluded that widespread exposure to secondhand smoke in the United States presents a serious and substantial public health risk.

Secondhand smoke is responsible for approximately 3,000 lung cancer deaths annually in nonsmokers in the United States. ETS is classified as a known human, or Group A, carcinogen under EPA's carcinogen assessment guidelines. This classification is reserved for those compounds or mixtures that show the strongest evidence of a cause-and-effect relationship in humans. Other agents classified by EPA as Group A carcinogens include radon, asbestos, and benzene, to name a few. Of these, ETS is the only one found to cause elevated cancer risks at commonly found indoor levels.

The report also includes the finding that secondhand smoke has subtle but significant other effects on the respiratory health of adult nonsmokers. These include coughing, phlegm production, chest discomfort, and reduced lung function.

Secondhand smoke is responsible for approximately 3,000 lung cancer deaths annually in nonsmokers in the United States.

Infants and young children whose parents smoke are among the most seriously affected by exposure to secondhand smoke. They experience an increased risk of lower respiratory tract infections such as pneumonia and bronchitis. EPA estimates that passive smoking is responsible for between 150,000 and 300,000 lower respiratory tract infections in infants and children under 18 months of age annually, resulting in between 7,500 and 15,000 hospitalizations each year. Children who have been exposed to secondhand smoke are also more likely to have reduced lung function and symptoms of respiratory irritation such as cough, excess phlegm, and wheezing. Passive smoking can lead to a buildup of fluid in the middle ear, the single most common cause of hospitalization of children for an operation.

Asthmatic children are especially at risk. EPA estimates that exposure to secondhand smoke increases the number of episodes and the severity of symptoms for between 200,000 and one million asthmatic children. Passive smoking is also a risk factor contributing to the development of new asthma cases in thousands of children each year.

EPA firmly believes that the scientific evidence is sufficient to warrant actions to protect nonsmokers from involuntary exposure to secondhand smoke. Accordingly, we are conducting a public outreach program to communicate the findings of the report to the public.

In July 1993, the Agency published a brochure, *What You Can Do About Secondhand Smoke*, which specifies actions that parents, decision makers, and building occupants can take to protect nonsmokers, including children, from indoor exposure to secondhand smoke. The brochure also contains a special message for smokers about how they can help protect people around them. Copies of the publication may be obtained by calling EPA's Indoor Air Quality Information Clearinghouse at 800-438-4318.

What kinds of actions are being advised? The following steps can help curb ETS exposure in the home, at child-care centers and schools, in the workplace, and in restaurants and bars:

- Don't smoke in your home or permit others to do so. If a family member smokes indoors, we recommend increasing ventilation in the area by opening windows or using exhaust fans. We also recommend that smoking should not occur if children are present, particularly infants and toddlers. Baby-sitters and others who work in the home should not be allowed to smoke indoors or near children.
- Every organization dealing with children—schools, day-care facilities, and other places where children spend time—should have a smoking policy that protects children from exposure to ETS.
- Every company should have a smoking policy that protects nonsmokers from involuntary exposure to tobacco smoke. Many businesses and organizations already have policies in place and more and more are instituting them, but these policies vary in their effectiveness. Simply separating smokers and nonsmokers within the same area, such as a cafeteria, will still expose nonsmokers to recirculated smoke and to smoke drifting in from smoking areas. Instead, companies should either prohibit smoking indoors or limit smoking to rooms that have been specially designed to prevent smoke from escaping to other areas of the building.
- If smoking is permitted in a restaurant or bar, smoking areas should be located in well-ventilated areas so nonsmokers will face less exposure. More and more restaurants and restaurant chains are prohibiting smoking in their facilities, and cities and counties across the United States are restricting smoking in restaurants within their jurisdictions.

EPA will be publishing guidance to help organizations establish smoking policies in indoor environments. Providing our children and the public with a smoke-free environment must be a national priority.

4

Tobacco Tax Increases Would Reduce Smoking

Liberty Aldrich

Liberty Aldrich is a former associate at the Advocacy Institute, a Washington, D.C.-based health and consumer advocacy organization, and is currently studying law at New York University.

The tobacco industry has succeeded in maintaining its profits, despite the large number of its customers who die each year, by recruiting hundreds of thousands of teenagers as new customers. The best way to discourage teenagers and others from smoking would be to increase taxes on cigarettes. The higher cost would deter many from smoking and the revenue generated could help pay for smokers' health care.

The tobacco industry has a problem: 435,000 of its most loyal customers die every year. Fortunately for the industry, the one million young people who light up for the first time each year more than compensate for this consumer drain. Our government has utterly failed to curtail this deadly cycle.

There is, however, a way out: increasing tobacco taxes will cause a drop in consumption of cigarettes, promoting health and providing revenue to help cover the real costs of smoking. These benefits will more than offset any disproportionate impact that the taxes will have on low-income communities—turning money spent on cigarettes into money spent on good health for everyone.

While the link between smoking and disease stands out as the starkest reason to discourage it through taxation, the strain that it places on our economy should not be shrugged off. Studies have found that the price of cigarettes reflects only a portion of the social cost of tobacco consumption. The remainder is "external" to the price, and consequently imposed on non-smoking society.

This external cost is analogous to the pollution a factory emits into its environment: If the factory is not forced to pay for the harm it causes, then it will not take that into account when it decides how much to produce. Likewise, our society does not force smokers to pay for—and thus consider—the full cost of their decision to smoke. The point is not to

Liberty Aldrich, "Butting Heads over the Tobacco Tax," *Dollars & Sense*, June 1993. Reprinted with permission. *Dollars & Sense* is a progressive economics magazine published ten times a year. First-year subscriptions cost $16.95 and may be ordered by writing *Dollars & Sense*, One Summer Street, Somerville, MA 02143 or by calling 617-628-2025.

make smokers pay for their sins; it is to send them a message, via a price tag, about the real consequences of their habit.

Medical costs are the most frequently cited, and perhaps most easily quantifiable, external costs of smoking. Thomas A. Hodgson, Chief Economist at the National Center for Health Statistics, conducted the most recent study comparing the medical expenditures of smokers to nonsmokers over their life cycles. Even without considering factors other than strictly medical costs, Hodgson got dramatic results: his most conservative estimate indicates that the population of smokers over the age of 25 in 1985 will incur $436 billion in medical costs in *excess* of those of nonsmokers, despite the smoker's early death.

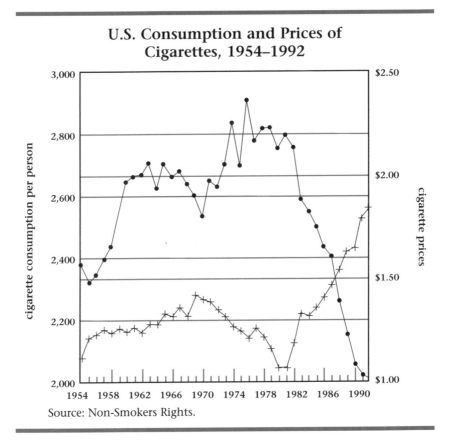

U.S. Consumption and Prices of Cigarettes, 1954–1992

Source: Non-Smokers Rights.

Calculations of smoking's cost to society are necessarily very complex and economists have gotten various results totaling up the bill. Proponents of tobacco tax increases frequently cite a 1985 Office of Technology Assessment (OTA) study which concluded that each pack of cigarettes costs $2.17 in external health-care and lost productivity costs. A team of economists led by Willard G. Manning of the University of Michigan criticized the OTA study in the *Journal of the American Medical Association*. Arguing that the OTA study was flawed by its failure to reflect the financial benefits that accrue to society when smokers die before they can collect all of their pension and social security benefits, Manning concluded that current levels of tobacco taxation cover smoking's costs.

The very idea that low prices can lead to deaths that are economically beneficial calls into question the economist's project. It is impossible for cheap tobacco to be a benefit to anyone except in the most theoretical economist's head.

On close inspection, the analysis of externalities splinters into question after question. One arises from the assumption that a "rational" actor decides which product he or she values most and proceeds to purchase that product: How can we assume that internalizing costs will send a clear message to a consumer when he or she may be acting according to the dictates of physical and mental addiction, which may not dovetail with his or her notion of the product's value? Another underlies any attempt to analyze externalities: Is it sufficient to simply internalize the cost of smoking into the price of a pack of cigarettes and call it a wash?

Studies may not provide the answer here. Calculating external costs can help us to render the economy more sensitive to health concerns, but it has serious limitations. The "internal" factors of death and disease—not externalities—must ultimately compel us to adopt a tax on tobacco.

How it works

A surprising number of smokers do overcome their addiction and make the economically rational decision: they quit when the price goes up. This decrease in consumption is the strongest argument for any tax on tobacco.

The chart reveals precisely how closely changes in price and consumption mirror each other. The American Lung Association has concluded that a 10% increase in cost leads to a 4% reduction in consumption. Increased price works especially well to reduce consumption among groups for whom price is an object—primarily the young and the economically disadvantaged. Teenagers have been shown to respond to fluctuations in price at three times the rate of adults.

There is data galore on this responsiveness. Several states have passed substantial tobacco taxes in the last several years. In 1988 voters ratified California's Proposition 99, which increased tobacco taxes by 25 cents a pack. Cigarette smoking subsequently dropped 17% between 1989 and 1991, about twice the national average. Canada's decision to sharply increase tobacco taxes in the 1980s—from 46 cents in 1980 to $3.27 in 1991—has had dramatic results: teen-smoking has been reduced by two-thirds. Any argument against tobacco taxes must confront the human implications of these statistics.

The real impact

Many specious arguments have been made in opposition to an increase in the tobacco tax—that it will spawn a "prohibitionesque" black market (virtually everywhere else, cigarettes are much more expensive than in the U.S., so there would be little supply for such a market), and that it will put millions out of work (a sound conversion strategy could solve this problem). But one criticism demands serious attention: that a tobacco tax is regressive. Like other consumption taxes, the tobacco tax would require low-income groups to pay proportionally more than rich people. However, flatfooted rejection of the tax on the grounds that it is regressive puts theory before reality, and turns a blind eye to the specifics of the tobacco situation.

Economists analyzing this question have by and large neglected to consider the overall impact of the tobacco tax, including reduced consumption and the accompanying health and economic benefits to low-income communities. Tobacco taxes save lives—a monumental benefit that distinguishes them from other taxes on consumer goods. In one attempt to fill out the picture, Joy Townsend concluded that, because low-income populations quit at a higher rate in response to price increases, tobacco taxes were actually progressive in the United Kingdom. A similar study has not yet been conducted in the United States.

Increasing tobacco taxes will cause a drop in consumption of cigarettes.

The tremendous financial and political power of the U.S. tobacco industry has enabled it to stave off taxes to a remarkable degree. As a percentage of pack price, the tobacco tax has dropped dramatically in the past forty years. According to the Tobacco Institute, taxes made up over 50% of the pack price in the late 1960s, and only slightly more than 25% in 1991. This failure to maintain the same percentage of taxes has left the industry plenty of room to raise cigarette prices at almost three times the rate of inflation. The profits reaped by tobacco companies through the sale of cigarettes are virtually unparalleled by profits on any other non-durable products. Philip Morris' recent decision to cut Marlboro's price by 40 cents per pack drew attention to just how much profit it was making—56 cents on each pack, or almost $5 billion a year.

The poor already suffer an unfair share of smoking's costs in this country because of the tobacco industry's clever "regressive" marketing techniques. Advertising directed at impoverished communities of color has recently ignited organized protests in those communities, but historically, it has met with little resistance and achieved its ends efficiently: 29% of blacks and 31% of Native Americans smoke, as compared to 26% of whites. The industry's favorite targets have little access to health information and care, but would quit in response to price increases. Finely printed messages on cigarette packs may pass unheeded, but a $5 price tag will not. Moreover, the government could earmark the revenue from a tobacco tax to pay for more direct, comprehensive health information for everyone.

Tobacco taxes provide a unique opportunity to tie revenues to programs that directly benefit low-income areas, thereby eliminating any regressive impact that is not already offset by reduced consumption. In California and Massachusetts, voter referenda tied tobacco tax revenue to a variety of such programs, including medical care for the poor.

Progressives oppose regressive taxation because it favors those who have over those who don't—but tobacco taxes benefit everyone. While they should not be considered a substitute for instituting a more equitable income tax code, neither should they be considered inimical to the goal of all progressive change: a fair distribution of society's resources. Health, too, is a resource, and one that our government can do a great deal more to spread around.

5

Regulating Nicotine as a Drug May Be Necessary

David A. Kessler

David A. Kessler is the commissioner of food and drugs for the Food and Drug Administration of the Department of Health and Human Services.

The Food and Drug Administration (FDA) regulates a substance as a drug if its producer intends the product to "affect the structure or any function of the body." The medical and scientific communities agree that nicotine, a primary ingredient in cigarettes, is addictive. New evidence indicates that cigarette manufacturers have long known about the addictive nature of nicotine, that they have developed the technology to manipulate nicotine levels in cigarettes, and that they may have used this technology to intentionally keep their consumers addicted to cigarettes. As a result of these findings, it may be time to regulate nicotine as a drug.

Editor's Note: The following testimony was delivered before the House Subcommittee on Health and the Environment on March 25, 1994.

The cigarette industry has attempted to frame the debate on smoking as the right of each American to choose. The question we must ask is whether smokers really have that choice.

Consider these facts:

- Two-thirds of adults who smoke say they wish they could quit.[1]
- Seventeen million try to quit each year, but fewer than one out of ten succeeds.[2] For every smoker who quits, nine try and fail.
- Three out of four adult smokers say that they are addicted.[3] By some estimates, as many as 74 to 90 percent are addicted.[4]
- Eight out of ten smokers say they wish they had never started smoking.[5]

Accumulating evidence suggests that cigarette manufacturers may intend this result—that they may be controlling smokers' choice by controlling the levels of nicotine in their products in a manner that creates and sustains an addiction in the vast majority of smokers.

That is the issue I am here to address: whether it is a choice by cigarette companies to maintain addictive levels of nicotine in their ciga-

Testimony of David A. Kessler before the U.S. House of Representatives Committee on Energy and Commerce, Subcommittee on Health and the Environment, March 25, 1994.

rettes, rather than a choice by consumers to continue smoking, that in the end is driving the demand for cigarettes in this country.

Although FDA [the Food and Drug Administration] has long recognized that the nicotine in tobacco produces drug-like effects, we never stepped in to regulate most tobacco products as drugs. One of the obstacles has been a legal one. A product is subject to regulation as a drug based primarily on its intended use. Generally, there must be an intent that the product be used either in relation to a disease or to affect the structure or function of the body. With certain exceptions,[6] we have not had sufficient evidence of such intent with regard to nicotine in tobacco products. Most people assume that the nicotine in cigarettes is present solely because it is a natural and unavoidable component of tobacco.

We now have cause to reconsider this historical view. The question now before us all is whether nicotine-containing cigarettes should be regulated as drugs. We seek guidance from the Congress on the public health and social issues that arise once the question is posed. This question arises today because of an accumulation of information in recent months and years. In my testimony today, I will describe some of that information.

The first body of information concerns the highly addictive nature of nicotine. The second body of information I will be talking about—in some detail—concerns the apparent ability of cigarette companies to control nicotine levels in cigarettes. We have information strongly suggesting that the amount of nicotine in a cigarette is there by design. Cigarette companies must answer the question: what is the real intent of this design?

Nicotine is highly addictive

Let me turn then to my first point about the addictive nature of nicotine.

The nicotine delivered by tobacco products is highly addictive. This was carefully documented in the 1988 Surgeon General's report. You can find nicotine's addictive properties described in numerous scientific papers.[7]

As with any addictive substance, some people can break their addiction to nicotine. But I doubt there is a person in this room who hasn't either gone to great pains to quit smoking, or watched a friend or relative struggle to extricate himself or herself from a dependence on cigarettes.

Remarkably, we see the grip of nicotine even among patients for whom the dangers of smoking could not be starker. After surgery for lung cancer, almost half of smokers resume smoking.[8] Among smokers who suffer a heart attack, 38 percent resume smoking while they are still in the hospital.[9] Even when a smoker has his or her larynx removed, 40 percent try smoking again.[10]

When a smoker sleeps, blood levels of nicotine decrease significantly. But the smoker doesn't need to be an expert on the concept of nicotine blood levels to know full well what that means. More than one-third of smokers reach for their first cigarette within 10 minutes of awakening;[11] nearly two-thirds smoke within the first half hour.[12] Experts in the field tell us that smoking the first cigarette of the day within 30 minutes of waking is a meaningful measure of addiction.[13]

I am struck especially by the statistics about our young people. A majority of adult smokers begin smoking as teenagers.[14] Unfortunately, 70 percent of young people ages 12–18 who smoke say that they believe that they are already dependent on cigarettes.[15] About 40 percent of high school seniors who smoke regularly have tried to quit and failed.[16]

It is fair to argue that the decision to start smoking may be a matter of choice. But once they have started smoking regularly, most smokers are in effect deprived of the choice to stop smoking. Recall one of the statistics I recited earlier. Seventeen million Americans try to quit smoking each year. But more than 15,000,000 individuals are unable to exercise that choice because they cannot break their addiction to cigarettes. My concern is that the choice that they are making at a young age quickly becomes little or no choice at all and will be very difficult to undo for the rest of their lives.

Nicotine is recognized as an addictive substance by such major medical organizations as the Office of U.S. Surgeon General, the World Health Organization,[17] the American Medical Association,[18] the American Psychiatric Association,[19] the American Psychological Association,[20] the American Society of Addiction Medicine,[21] and the Medical Research Council in the United Kingdom.[22] All of these organizations acknowledge tobacco use as a form of drug dependence or addiction with severe adverse health consequences.

Definitions of an addictive substance may vary slightly, but they all embody some key criteria: first, compulsive use, often despite knowing the substance is harmful; second, a psychoactive effect—that is, a direct chemical effect in the brain; third, what researchers call reinforcing behavior that conditions continued use.[27] In addition, withdrawal symptoms occur with many drugs and occur in many cigarette smokers who try to quit. These are hallmarks of an addictive substance and nicotine meets them all.

When a smoker inhales, once absorbed in the bloodstream, nicotine is carried to the brain in only 7–9 seconds,[23] setting off a biological chain reaction that is critical in establishing and reinforcing addiction.

Accumulating evidence suggests that cigarette manufacturers . . . may be controlling smokers' choice by controlling the levels of nicotine.

Over the past few years, scientists have generated a tremendous amount of information on the similarities among different addictive substances. Some crucial information has come from the fact that, in a laboratory setting, animals will self-administer addictive substances. This self-administration may involve the animal pushing a lever or engaging in other actions to get repeated doses of the addictive substance. With very few exceptions, animals will self-administer those drugs that are considered highly addictive in humans, including morphine and cocaine, and will not self-administer those drugs that are not considered addictive.[24, 25]

Understanding that animals will self-administer addictive substances has fundamentally changed the way that scientists view addiction in humans.[24] It has turned attention away from the concept of an "addictive personality" to a realization that addictive drugs share common chemical effects in the brain.[24]

Despite the wide chemical diversity among different addictive substances, a property that most of them share is the ability to affect the regulation of a chemical called dopamine in parts of the brain that are important to emotion and motivation.[26] It is now believed that it is the effect of addictive substances on dopamine that is responsible for driving animals to self-administer these substances and for causing humans to develop addictions.[24]

Regulation of dopamine rewards the activity and causes the animal or person to repeat the activity that produced that reward.[24, 26] The process by which the regulation of dopamine leads an animal or a human to repeat the behavior is known as "reinforcement."[24] Drugs that have the ability to directly modify dopamine levels can produce powerfully ingrained addictive behavior.[24]

One of the ways that researchers now test the addictive properties of drugs is to determine whether animals will self-administer that substance and then to determine whether the animals will stop self-administering if the chemical action of the substance is blocked by the simultaneous administration of another drug that prevents the first substance from acting in the brain. Data gathered over the past 15 years have documented that laboratory animals will voluntarily self-administer nicotine;[25,27] that nicotine does stimulate the release of dopamine;[28] and that laboratory animals will decrease self-administration of nicotine if the action of nicotine, or the release of dopamine, in the brain is blocked.[29, 30]

A number of top tobacco industry officials have stated that they do not believe that tobacco is addictive.[31] They may tell you that smokers smoke for "pleasure," not to satisfy a nicotine craving. Experts tell us that their patients report that only a small minority of the cigarettes they smoke in a day are highly pleasurable.[32] Experts believe that the remainder are smoked primarily to sustain nicotine blood levels and to avoid withdrawal symptoms.[32]

The industry couches nicotine's effects in euphemisms such as "satisfaction" or "impact" or "strength." Listen to what they say in one company's patent:

> It also has been generally recognized that the smoker's perception
> of the "strength" of the cigarette is directly related to the amount
> of nicotine contained in the cigarette smoke during each puff.[33]

But these terms only sidestep the fact that the companies are marketing a powerfully addictive agent. Despite the buzzwords used by industry, what smokers are addicted to is not "rich aroma' or "pleasure" or "satisfaction." What they are addicted to is nicotine, pure and simple, because of its psychoactive effects and its drug dependence qualities.

To smokers who know that they are addicted, to those who have buried a loved one who was addicted, it is simply no longer credible to deny the highly addictive nature of nicotine.

Controlling the level of nicotine in cigarettes

My second point involves a growing body of information about the control of nicotine levels exercised by the tobacco industry. I do not have all the facts or all the answers today. The picture is still incomplete. But from a number of pieces of information, from a number of sources, a picture of tobacco company practices is beginning to emerge.

The public thinks of cigarettes as simply blended tobacco rolled in paper. But they are much more than that. Some of today's cigarettes may, in fact, qualify as high technology nicotine delivery systems that deliver nicotine in precisely calculated quantities—quantities that are more than sufficient to create and to sustain addiction in the vast majority of individuals who smoke regularly.

But you don't have to take it from me. Consider how people in the tobacco industry itself view cigarettes.

Just take a moment to look at the excerpts from an internal memorandum written by a supervisor of research that circulated in the Philip Morris Company in 1972:

> Think of the cigarette pack as a storage container for a day's supply of nicotine. . . . Think of the cigarette as a dispenser for a dose unit of nicotine. . . . Think of a puff of smoke as the vehicle for nicotine. . . . Smoke is beyond question the most optimized vehicle of nicotine and the cigarette the most optimized dispenser of smoke.

"Dispensers of smoke . . . which is a vehicle for delivering nicotine." This quote is a revealing self-portrait.

Or listen to the words in one tobacco company patent:

> Medical research has established that nicotine is the active ingredient in tobacco. Small doses of nicotine provide the user with certain pleasurable effects resulting in the desire for additional doses.[34]

The design of cigarettes

How does this industry design cigarettes?

The history of the tobacco industry is a story of how a product that may at one time have been a simple agricultural commodity appears to have become a nicotine delivery system. Prior to the 1940s, the waste products from cigarettes—the stems, the scraps, and the dust—were discarded. The tobacco industry had identified no use for these materials in the cigarette manufacturing process.

Then, in the 1940s and '50s, the industry created reconstituted tobacco from the previously unusable tobacco stems, scraps, and dust. This gave cigarette makers the ability to reduce the cost of producing cigarettes by using fewer tobacco leaves and making up the difference by using reconstituted tobacco. While the motive appeared to be purely economic, the reconstitution process was nevertheless a critical development that started the industry down the path toward controlling and manipulating nicotine levels. The ability to control and manipulate nicotine levels becomes important in light of another key realization. Industry patents show that the industry recognized that nicotine is the active ingredient in tobacco smoke. It is what produces the psychoactive effects that lead smokers to crave cigarettes.

Most people assume that the nicotine in cigarettes is present solely because it is a natural and unavoidable component of tobacco.

Numerous patents illustrate how the industry has been working to sustain the psychoactive effects of nicotine in cigarettes. [The author displays] samples from several categories of patents: eight patents to increase nicotine content by adding nicotine to the tobacco rod; five patents to increase nicotine content by adding nicotine to filters, wrappers and other parts of the cigarette; three patents that use advanced technology to manipulate the levels of nicotine in tobacco; eight patents on extraction of nicotine from tobacco; and nine patents to develop new chemical variants of nicotine.

Patents not only describe a specific invention. They also speak to the industry's capabilities, to its research, and provide insight into what it may be attempting to achieve with its products.

It is prudent to keep in mind that patents do not necessarily tell us what processes are currently being used in manufacturing cigarettes. Nevertheless, the number and pattern of these patents leaves little doubt that the cigarette industry has developed enormously sophisticated methods for manipulating nicotine levels in cigarettes. Today, a cigarette company can add or subtract nicotine from tobacco. It can set nicotine levels. In many cigarettes today, the amount of nicotine present is a result of choice, not chance.

Let me show you the language in some of these patents. This is in the industry's own words.

Listen to what industry says it *wants* to be able to do with nicotine.

First, the industry wants precise *control* of the amount of nicotine in cigarettes to provide desired physiological effects:

> Maintaining the nicotine content at a sufficiently high level to provide the desired physiological activity, taste, and odor . . . can thus be seen to be a significant problem in the tobacco art.[35]

Second, the industry wants to *increase* the amount of nicotine in some cigarettes.

> . . . the perceived taste or strength of the cigarettes classified as having lower levels of "tar" and nicotine are progressively less than that of the cigarettes which are classified as approaching the characteristics of the "full flavor" cigarettes. It has been proposed to add nicotine and other flavorants to the cut filler of the lower "tar" cigarettes to enhance the taste, strength, and satisfaction of such cigarettes.[36]

> This invention . . . concerns the problem of maintaining or increasing the nicotine content of the smoke whilst avoiding an undesirable level of particulate matter in the smoke. . . .[37]

Now listen to what the industry says it can do, right now, at least for patent purposes, with the nicotine in cigarettes:

It can precisely *manipulate nicotine levels* in cigarettes:

> This invention permits the release into tobacco smoke, in controlled amounts, of desirable flavorants, as well as the release, in controlled amounts and when desired, of nicotine into tobacco smoke.[38]

> It is another object of the invention to provide an agent for the treatment of tobacco smoke whereby nicotine is easily released thereinto in controlled amounts.[39]

> [I]t can be seen that the process . . . enables the manipulation of the nicotine content of tobacco material, such as cut leaf and reconstituted leaf, by removal of nicotine from a suitable nicotine tobacco source or by the addition of nicotine to a low nicotine tobacco material.[40]

> . . . processed tobaccos can be manufactured under conditions suitable to provide products having various nicotine levels.[41]

Examples of suitable tobacco materials include . . . processed tobacco materials such as expanded tobaccos, processed tobacco stems, reconstituted tobacco materials or reconstituted tobacco materials having varying levels of endogenous and exogenous nicotine. . . .[42]

. . . the present invention . . . is particularly useful for the maintenance of the proper amount of nicotine in tobacco smoke.

. . . previous efforts have been made to add nicotine to tobacco products wherein the nicotine level in the tobacco was undesirably low.[43]

It can precisely *manipulate the rate* at which the nicotine is delivered in the cigarette:

It is a further object of this invention to provide a cigarette which delivers a larger amount of nicotine in the first few puffs of the cigarette than in the last few puffs.[44]

It can *transfer nicotine from one material to another* at will:

Moreover, the process is useful for transferring naturally occurring nicotine from tobacco having a generally high nicotine content to a nicotine deficient tobacco, tobacco filler materials, or RL (reconstituted leaf) which are used in the production of cigarettes and other smoking products. . . . [A] low nicotine tobacco . . . can also be used as the nicotine donor. . . .[45]

It is another object of this invention to provide a process for the migration of nicotine from one tobacco substrate (leaf material or reconstituted leaf) to a second tobacco substrate (leaf material, reconstituted leaf material or tobacco stems) or to a non-tobacco substrate.[46]

It can *increase* the amount of nicotine in cigarettes:

If desired, nicotine can be incorporated into the expansion solvents used to provide a volume expanded processed tobacco material having a high nicotine content.[47]

The present invention provides a nicotine-enhanced smoking device with a high nicotine release efficiency. . . .Thus, the smoker is provided with more nicotine from the nicotine-enhanced device than from a similar smoking device which does not contain the nicotine solution or from a comparable cigarette.[48]

The present invention is concerned with the application of additives, such as . . . physiologically active agents such as nicotine components to the smoking rod, in order to improve or help to improve the satisfaction provided to the smoker.[49]

It can *add nicotine to any part* of the cigarette:

The salts [nicotine levulinate] can be incorporated into the smoking article in a variety of places or sites. For example, the salt can be applied to the filler material, incorporated within some or all of the filler material, applied to the wrapper of the tobacco rod, applied within the glue line of the wrapper of the tobacco rod, applied within a region (e.g., a cavity). . . .[50]

It can use a variety of methods to add nicotine to tobacco:

. . . [T]he additive [nicotine levulinate] can be applied using syringes or techniques such as spraying, electrostatic deposition, impregnation, garniture injection, spray drying, inclusion and encapsulation technologies, and the like.[51]

Let me describe in some detail how some of the technologies can be used to increase or control the nicotine level of tobacco.

The industry had to tackle a new problem beginning in the 1960s as public concern about the health consequences of smoking intensified. The industry began to market cigarettes it described as low yield. It faced a major challenge, however, because in the words of patent no. 4,830,028, "the perceived taste or strength of the cigarettes classified as having lower levels of 'tar' and nicotine are progressively less than that of the cigarettes which are classified as approaching the characteristics of the 'full flavor' cigarettes."

The patent then describes a way to add nicotine to the "low yield" cigarettes. If nicotine alone is sprayed on a blend of tobacco, the patent states that the smoke that results will be unacceptably harsh or irritating to the user. So, instead of just spraying nicotine on the tobacco blend, the patent combines nicotine with another compound, an organic acid called levulinic acid, to form a salt that masks the irritating qualities of nicotine. The patent demonstrates that different percentages of the nicotine salt can be added to blends of tobacco to produce different nicotine concentrations. The control cigarette, the one without any added nicotine, contains 1.66 percent nicotine. Adding 1 percent nicotine salt results in a cigarette with 2.05 percent nicotine. As one increases the amount of nicotine salt sprayed on the tobacco blend, the nicotine content of the tobacco increases.

In this process, great care is paid to the pH of the smoke because pH affects the bioavailability of nicotine—that is, how much the body absorbs. The patent demonstrates the technology to increase nicotine content in tobacco by up to 76 percent.

Once they have started smoking regularly, most smokers are in effect deprived of the choice to stop smoking.

U.S. patent no. 5,065,775 describes another technology that can control the nicotine content of tobacco filler. This involves a process for "modifying the alkaloid content of a tobacco material and, in particular, for providing a processed tobacco material having a controlled nicotine content." (C2:57-60) In the words of the patent, "[t]he process of the present invention provides a skilled artisan with an efficient and effective method for changing the character of a tobacco material (e.g., rearranging components of a tobacco material or altering the chemical nature or composition of a tobacco material) in a controlled manner. That is, the process . . . can be employed in a way such that changes in the chemical composition of tobacco can be monitored as to occur to a desired degree." (C3:55-63)

The patent allows for the removal of selected substances from tobacco, and incorporating controlled amounts of substances into tobacco. Example 4 within this patent shows how a tobacco blend that starts off with a 2.3 percent nicotine content can end up with a 5.2 percent nicotine content. A highly concentrated nicotine solution is created by subjecting a tobacco blend to a series of chemical steps, including adding water, removing solids, increasing the pH, and mixing this substance with chlorofluorocarbon (CFC) 11 and then evaporating off that CFC 11. This concentrate is then added to water-washed tobacco to increase its nicotine content. This patent demonstrates the technology to increase the nicotine content in tobacco by more than 100 percent.

What smokers are addicted to is not "rich aroma" or "pleasure" or "satisfaction." What they are addicted to is nicotine.

A third example of sophisticated technology involves the direct transfer of nicotine from one type of tobacco to another type of tobacco. U.S. patent no. 4,898,188 utilizes supercritical fluid extraction. In example 2 in the patent, liquid carbon dioxide is used to transfer nicotine from Burley cut tobacco filler to flue-cured cut tobacco. The flue-cured cut filler starts off with a nicotine content of 2.59 percent and ends up with a nicotine content of 4.83 percent. The Burley cut filler starts off with a nicotine content of 3.56 percent and ends with a nicotine content of 0.88 percent. This patent demonstrates that nicotine can be transferred in significant amounts from one type of tobacco filler to another.

Additional information about the ability to set nicotine content at varying levels comes from the following ad, headlined "More Nicotine or Less," which appeared in an international tobacco trade publication:

> Nicotine levels are becoming a growing concern to the designers of modern cigarettes, particularly those with lower "tar" deliveries. The Kimberly-Clark tobacco reconstitution process used by LTR Industries permits adjustments of nicotine to your exact requirements. These adjustments will not affect the other important properties of customized reconstituted tobacco produced at LTR Industries: low tar delivery, high filling power, high yield, and the flexibility to convey organoleptic modifications. We can help you control your tobacco.

In fact the process described in this advertisement can raise the level of nicotine beyond what is naturally found in tobacco materials, especially the stems and scraps. A 1985 tobacco journal article describing the LTR process states

> Though standard reconstituted tobacco products contain 0.7–1.0 percent nicotine, LTR Industries offers the possibility of increasing the nicotine content of the final sheet to a maximum of 3.5 percent. . . .

> A dramatic increase in tobacco taste and smoke body is noted in the nicotine-fortified reconstituted tobacco.[52]

All of this apparent technology for manipulating nicotine in tobacco products raises the question of how the industry determines how much nicotine should be in various products. More importantly, since the technology apparently exists to reduce nicotine in cigarettes to insignificant levels,[53, 54] why, one is led to ask, does the industry keep nicotine in cigarettes at all?

The tobacco industry would like you to believe that all it is doing is returning the nicotine that is removed during the process of producing reconstituted tobacco. It should be clear from what I have described thus far that the technology the industry may have available goes beyond such modest efforts.

The industry may also tell you that it is adjusting nicotine levels to be consistent with established "FTC yields"—these are the amounts of tar, nicotine, and carbon monoxide that are measured for each cigarette product by smoking machines, and disclosed under a voluntary agreement with the Federal Trade Commission. In fact, the control of nicotine levels in cigarettes, dating back at least to patents granted in 1966 for adjusting nicotine levels, preceded the first rules adopted by the FTC on disclosing tar and nicotine yields. Moreover, there is nothing about the FTC yields that would require tobacco companies to increase nicotine in low tar cigarettes, as the industry patents suggest they do. There are no FTC restrictions on nicotine levels, and the FTC guidelines take into account crop variability by sampling completed cigarettes from 50 retail outlets across the country. Indeed, there is no FTC restriction that would prevent the industry from reducing nicotine below addicting levels or eliminating it altogether.

The cigarette industry has developed enormously sophisticated methods for manipulating nicotine levels in cigarettes.

In fact, the technology reflected in the cigarette industry's patents appears to be intended to allow the industry to set the nicotine content of tobacco products at defined levels that have little to do with either the amount of nicotine that was removed during the processing of the tobacco, or with the simple goal of maintaining consistency with established FTC yields. The technology may exist to allow the industry to set nicotine levels wherever it wants or in fact to remove nicotine entirely. With all the apparent advances in technology, why do the nicotine levels found in the vast majority of cigarettes remain at addictive levels?

Nicotine levels may be dictated in part by marketing strategies and demographics. A blatant example comes from information on the marketing of smokeless tobacco. There is evidence that smokeless tobacco products with lower amounts of nicotine are marketed as "starter" products for new users, and that advertising is used to encourage users to "graduate" to products with higher levels of nicotine. The evidence was developed in lawsuits brought against one manufacturer of smokeless tobacco.

The tobacco industry may tell you that nicotine is important in cigarettes solely for "flavor." There is a great deal of information that suggests otherwise. Some of the patents specifically distinguish nicotine from flavorants.[55] An RJR book on flavoring tobacco, while listing around a thousand flavorants, fails to list nicotine as a flavoring agent.[56] Even research scientists from the same company acknowledge that the nicotine in cigarettes provides pharmacological and psychological effects to smokers in addition to any mere sensory effects.[57]

Moreover, the available information shows that the industry has gone to significant lengths to develop technologies to mask the flavor of increased levels in cigarettes. As I have already noted, the industry's own patents reveal that increasing nicotine in fact usually produces an unacceptably harsh and irritating product, and that the industry has had to take special steps to mask the flavor of increased nicotine in low tar cigarettes.

This should not come as a surprise. The Merck Index, the authoritative encyclopedia of chemicals, describes nicotine as having "an acrid, burning taste." Webster's 7th New Collegiate Dictionary defines acrid as "sharp and harsh or unpleasantly pungent in taste or odor; irritating, corrosive." In fact, U.S. patent no. 4,620,554 uses the word "hazardous" to describe the taste of nicotine.

What appears to be true is that smokers become accustomed to, and associate, the sensory impact of nicotine (burning in the throat) with the resulting psychoactive effects of nicotine, and thus look for those sensory signals in a cigarette; this is called "conditioned reinforcement."[58]

Moreover, if nicotine is just another flavorant in tobacco, why not use a substitute ingredient with comparable flavor, but without the addictive potential? For example, it has been repeatedly shown that substitute ingredients, such as hot pepper (capsaicin)[59] and citric acid,[60] have similar irritating sensory effects.

Similarities to the pharmaceutical industry

This kind of sophistication in setting levels of a physiologically active substance suggests that what we are seeing in the cigarette industry more and more resembles the actions of a pharmaceutical manufacturer. Besides controlling the amount of a physiologically active ingredient, there are a number of other similarities.

One similarity between the cigarette industry and the pharmaceutical industry is the focus on bioavailability. Bioavailability is the rate and extent that pharmacologically active substances get into the bloodstream. For example, the pH of tobacco smoke affects the bioavailability of nicotine.[61] The tobacco industry has conducted research on the pH of smoke[62] and has undertaken to control the pH in tobacco smoke. In patent examples, chemicals have been added to tobacco to affect the pH of tobacco smoke.[63] The industry has even performed bioavailability and pharmacokinetic studies on conventional and novel cigarettes.[64]

The cigarette industry has undertaken research to look at the specific activity of added versus naturally occurring nicotine.[65] Additional research looked at the differences between spiking, spraying and blending compounds into cigarettes.[66]

Development of an "express" cigarette, a shorter, faster burning cigarette with the same amount of tar and nicotine, has been reported in the lay press recently. This is another example of how cigarette companies appear to be controlling the amounts of nicotine to deliver set levels.[67]

The tobacco industry would like you to believe that all it is doing is returning the nicotine that is removed during the process of producing reconstituted tobacco.

The cigarette industry has also undertaken a significant amount of research looking at the potential "beneficial" effects of nicotine. It has studied the effects of nicotine on anxiety, heart rate, electroencephalographs (EEGs), and behavioral performance tasks. Such research on the physiological effects of an active ingredient is a common part of pharmaceutical drug development.[68, 69, 70, 71, 72, 73, 74, 75]

Perhaps the most striking aspect of the research undertaken by the tobacco industry is its search for, and its patenting of, new nicotine-like chemicals that exhibit pharmacological properties which, in their own words, "are indicated for utility as potential psychotherapeutic agents."[76] One patent describes nicotine-like chemicals which

> exhibit tranquilizing and muscle-relaxing properties when administered to mammals. The nicotine analogs do not exhibit nicotine-like properties, such as tachycardia, hypertension, gastrointestinal effects, emesis in dogs, and the like.

Example XXIX in the patent

> illustrates the pharmacological properties of nicotine analogs. . . .

> The tranquilizing effects of invention nicotine compounds are measured after intraperitoneal (IP) and intraventricular (IVC) administration in the form of hydrochloride salts.

> Sedation is determined by measuring locomotion in an open field maze, and the response to noxious (air blast) stimuli. Body tone is estimated by handling rats and by the ability to hang from a rotating rod.

> Tranquilization after intraventricular (IVC injection) is estimated from muscle weakness in all four limbs, body tone and general activity.[77]

The problem of the low-yield cigarette

We at the Food and Drug Administration are concerned not only about the control over nicotine levels exercised by the cigarette industry, we are also concerned that the problems associated with nicotine are aggravated by significant limitations in consumers' ability to reduce their exposure to nicotine by selecting "low" nicotine cigarettes.

Most people who smoke low yield or "light" cigarettes believe that they are getting less nicotine and tar by smoking these cigarettes. For the last 25 years the American public has relied on FTC ratings of tar and nicotine in advertising to tell them what they will be consuming. The "FTC method" utilizes a machine that tests cigarettes in a process involving a two-second, 35 milliliter puff each minute until a predetermined butt length is reached.[78]

Most people don't realize that low yield cigarettes, as determined by the FTC method, do not usually result in proportionally less nicotine being absorbed when compared to high yield cigarettes.[79] Furthermore, there is little correlation between low yield FTC ratings and the total amount of nicotine in cigarettes.[80]

It is a myth that people who smoke low nicotine cigarettes are necessarily going to get less nicotine than people who smoke high nicotine cigarettes. There are several reasons for this. One reason is that there are differences between the smoking habits of a machine and a human. The way in which a cigarette is smoked is probably the most important determinant of how much tar and nicotine is inhaled. Humans can compensate—and do compensate—when smoking low yield cigarettes, by altering puff volume, puff duration, inhalation frequency, depth of inhalation, number of cigarettes smoked.[81, 82, 83, 84, 85, 86, 87] As a result of these compensatory mechanisms, a low yield cigarette can actually result in a relatively high intake of nicotine.[88]

Beyond the human compensatory mechanisms, several other factors under manufacturers' control contribute to a lowering of machine ratings. These factors include the positioning of ventilation holes, how fast the cigarette paper burns, and the length of the filter paper overwrap.[91]

To understand how the position of ventilation holes in a cigarette can confound the FTC ratings, it is important to recognize that the main determinants of whether a cigarette has a high or low yield in machine testing are the cigarette's ventilation and burning characteristics.[89] Most low yield cigarettes achieve their low ratings because of filter characteristics and also because the smoke is diluted with air. The air dilution is accomplished in part by placing ventilation holes in the filter. What scientists have demonstrated is that "although smoking machines which measure tar and nicotine do not occlude the perforations," 32–69 percent of low tar smokers have blocked the holes with their fingers or lips, resulting in larger nicotine yields.[90] The ventilation holes are sometimes laser generated and can be hard for the smoker to see. Not all smokers are aware of the existence of these holes or that the smoker may be blocking them.

Two other factors that are under manufacturers' control can also confound the usefulness of the FTC ratings. The FTC method smokes a cigarette down to within 3 millimeters of the tipping paper overwrap. According to one study, "between 1967 and 1978, 18 brands of filter cigarettes underwent increases in overwrap width that reduced the amount of tobacco smoked in the cigarettes on the machine, even though the remaining tobacco is still smokeable."[91] Another way that the FTC numbers can be confounded is by "increasing the rate at which cigarettes burn." A faster burning cigarette lowers the puff count. Manufacturers can increase the rate at which a cigarette burns by controlling the porosity of the cigarette paper. The machine takes a puff every minute, but humans can adjust their smoking rate.[91]

Because of all these confounding factors we are concerned that consumers may assume that low yield cigarettes in fact deliver low tar and nicotine when in reality they do not.

Actual nicotine levels in cigarettes

To assess the levels of nicotine in cigarettes, we did two things. First, FDA laboratories measured the amount of nicotine actually in several types of cigarettes. We analyzed three varieties of one brand family of cigarettes; one that is regular, one that is low tar, and one that is ultra low. What surprised us was that the variety advertised as having the lowest yield in fact had the highest concentration of nicotine in the cigarette.

Second, we formally requested from our colleagues at the Federal Trade Commission summary information derived from their data base on the levels of nicotine in cigarettes. What we found was that since 1982 (the earliest year for which the computer data base is available), the sales-weighted levels of FTC nicotine in cigarettes appear to increase. What was equally striking was that when we segmented sales into high tar, low tar, and ultra low tar cigarettes, the nicotine/tar ratio was higher in the ultra low tar group. We would not have expected to see these differences because high tar has usually been associated with high nicotine, low tar has usually been associated with low nicotine. It has often been said that tar and nicotine travel together in the cigarette smoke. The disparities in the nicotine/tar ratios among these varieties raise the question as to how this can occur.

The next task facing the FDA is to determine whether nicotine-containing cigarettes are "drugs" within the meaning of the Federal Food, Drug, and Cosmetic Act.

Our inquiry is necessarily shaped by the definition of "drug" in the Act. It is a definition that focuses on "vendor intent." More specifically, it focuses primarily on whether the vendor intends the product to "affect the structure or any function of the body."

The evidence we have presented today suggests that cigarette manufacturers may intend that most smokers buy cigarettes to satisfy their nicotine addiction.

We do not yet have all the evidence necessary to establish cigarette manufacturers' intent. It should be clear, however, that in determining intent what cigarette manufacturers say can be less important than what they do. The fact that the technology may be available to reduce the nicotine to less than addictive levels is relevant in determining manufacturer intent.

It is important to note that the possibility of FDA's exerting jurisdiction over cigarettes raises many broader public health and social issues for Congress to contemplate. There is the possibility that regulation of the nicotine in cigarettes as drugs would result in the removal of nicotine-containing cigarettes from the market, limiting the amount of nicotine in cigarettes to levels that are not addictive, or otherwise restricting access to them, unless the industry could show that nicotine-containing cigarettes are safe and effective. If nicotine were removed, the nation would face a host of issues involving the withdrawal from addiction that would be experienced by millions of Americans who smoke.

There is, of course, the issue of black market cigarettes. With nicotine, as with other powerfully addicting substances, a black market could develop.

In these issues, we seek guidance from Congress.

The one thing that I think is certain is that it is time for all of us—for the FDA, for the Congress, for the American public—to learn more about the way cigarettes are designed today and the results of the tobacco industry's own research on the addictive properties of nicotine.

Notes

1. Thomas, R.M., Larsen, M.D. Smoking Prevalence, Beliefs, and Activities by Gender and Other Demographic Indicators. Princeton, NJ: The Gallup Organization, Inc., 1993.

2. MMWR. July 9, 1993.

3. Thomas, R.M., Larsen, M.D. Smoking Prevalence, Beliefs, and Activities by Gender and Other Demographic Indicators. Princeton, NJ: The Gallup Organization, Inc., 1993.

4. Hughes et al. Prevalence of tobacco dependence and withdrawal, 1987; 205-208.

5. Thomas, R.M., Larsen, M.D. Smoking Prevalence, Beliefs, and Activities by Gender and Other Demographic Indicators. Princeton, NJ: The Gallup Organization, Inc., 1993.

6. United States v. 46 Cartons . . . Fairfax Cigarettes, 113 F. Supp. 336 (D.N.J. 1953); United States v. 354 Bulk Cartons Trim Reducing-Aid Cigarettes, 178 F. Supp. 847 (D. N. J. 1959).

7. 1994 Surgeon General's Report. Nicotine Addiction in Adolescence. Health Consequences.

Benowitz, N.L. Pharmacologic Aspects of Cigarette Smoking and Nicotine Addiction. NEJM 1988, No. 17:1318.

Benowitz, N.L. Cigarette Smoking and Nicotine Addiction. Medical Clinics of North America. Vol. 76, No. 2, March 1992.

Henningfield, J.E., Nemeth-Coslett, R. Nicotine Dependence: Interface between Tobacco and Tobacco-related Disease. Chest. Vol. 93: 37S-55S, 1988.

U.S. Department of Health and Human Services. Drug Abuse and Drug Abuse Research: The Third Triennial Report to Congress from the Secretary, Department of Health and Human Services, 1991.

Schelling, T.C. Addictive Drugs: The Cigarette Experience. Science. Vol:255.

Jones, R.T. Tobacco Dependence. Psychopharmacology: The Third Generation of Progress, pg.1589, 1987.

8. Davison and Duffy. Smoking habits of long term survivors of surgery for lung cancer. Thorax 1982,37:331-333.

9. Bigelow et al. Smoking cessation and relapse among cardiac patients. Relapse and Recovery in Drug Abuse; NIDA Research Monograph 72 1986:167-171.

10. West and Himbury. Smoking habits after laryngectomy. Br. Med Journal, 1985, 291:514-515.

11. Gary Giovino. Report to FDA from CDC National Center for Health Statistics. National health interview survey, 1987.

12. Gary Giovino. Report to FDA from CDC National Center for Health Statistics. National health interview survey, 1987.

13. Gary Giovino. FDA interview with CDC. March 1994. Hughes et al. Prevalence of tobacco dependence and withdrawal. Am J Psychiatry, 1987, 205-208.

14. U.S. Department of Health and Human Services, Public Health Service, Centers for Disease Control and Prevention, National Center for Chronic Disease Prevention and Health Promotion, Office on Smoking and Health. Preventing Tobacco Use Among Young People: A Report of the Surgeon General, 1994; pg. 67.

15. U.S. Department of Health and Human Services. Preventing tobacco use among young people: A report of the Surgeon General, 1994; pg. 95.

16. U.S. Department of Health and Human Services. Preventing tobacco use among young people: A report of the Surgeon General, 1994.

17. World Health Organization. Smokeless tobacco control. Technical Report Series 773, 1988.

World Health Organization. Women and tobacco, 1992; 33-34.

18. American Medical Association. 1993 AMA Policy Compendium. 30,958; pg. 35.

19. American Psychiatric Association. Diagnostic and Statistical Manual of Mental Disorders. Third edition revised, 1987; 150-51 and 181-82.

20. The American Psychological Association. Statement before the U.S.

House of Representatives Committee on Energy and Commerce Subcommittee on Health and the Environment, July 29, 1988.

21. The Royal Society of Canada. Tobacco, Nicotine and Addiction. The Health Protection Branch Health and Welfare Canada, August 31, 1989.

22. Medical Research Council Field Review. The basis of drug dependence, January 1994; 1-13.

23. Henningfield et al. Drug and alcohol dependence, 1993:23-29 citing Benowitz, N.L., National Institute of Drug Abuse Research Monograph; 12-29.

24. Gardner, Eliot L. Brain Reward Mechanisms. Substance Abuse: A Comprehensive Textbook. Second Edition. William and Wilkens, 1992.

25. Yokel, R. Intravenous self-administration: Response rates, the effects of pharmacological challenges, and drug preference: Methods of Assessing the Reinforcing Properties of Abused Drugs. Springer-Verlag, 1987.

26. DiChiara, G. and Imperato, A. Drugs abused by humans preferentially increase synaptic dopamine concentrations in the mesolimbic system of freely moving rats. Proceedings of the National Academy of Sciences. Vol. 85, July 1988:5274-78.

27. Department of Health and Human Services, Public Health Service. The Health Consequences of Smoking: Nicotine Addiction. A report of the Surgeon General. DHHS (CDC) 1988. Publication no: 88-8406.

28. Imperato, A., Mulas A., and DiChiara, G. Nicotine preferentially stimulates dopamine release in the limbic system of freely moving rats. European Journal of Pharmacology, 1986; 132:337-338.

29. Corrigall, W.A., Franklin, K.B.J., Coen, K.M. and P.B.S. Clarke. The mesolimbic dopaminergic system is implicated in the reinforcing effects of nicotine. Psychopharmacology, 1992; 107:285-289.

30. Corrigall, W.A. and Coen, K.M. Selective dopamine antagonists reduce nicotine self-administration. Psychopharmacology, 1991; 104: 171-176 .

31. Robinson J.H. and Pritchard, W.S. The role of nicotine in tobacco use. Psychopharmacology, 1992; 108:397-407.

Rosenblatt, R. How do they live with themselves? New York Times Magazine, March 20, 1994.

32. Henningfield, J.E., Schiffman, S. Informal communications.

33. U.S. patent no. 4,595,024 C1:33-36.

34. U.S. patent no. 4,676,259 C1:21-24.

35. U.S. patent no. 3,280,823 C1:43-48.

36. U.S. patent no. 4,830,028 C1:40-47.

37. U.S. patent no. 3,861,400 C1:1-10

38. U.S. patent no. 3,280,823 C2:37-40.

39. U.S. patent no. 3,584,630 C2:69-71.

40. U.S. patent no. 4,215,706 C3:61-66.

41. U.S. patent no. 5,031,646 C5:63-65.

42. U.S. patent no. 5,031,646 C5:21-27.

43. U.S. patent no. 3,584,630 C2:5-15.

44. U.S. patent no. 4,595,024 C2:23-26.

45. U.S. patent no. 4,215,706 C1:40-48.

46. U.S. patent no. 5,018,540 C2:39-43.

47. U.S. patent no. 5,031,646 C5:65-68.

48. U.S. patent no. 4,676,259 C2:30-33, 53-56.

49. U.S. patent no. 4,236,532 C1:35-40.

50. U.S. patent no. 4,830,028 C5:59-65.

51. U.S. patent no. 4,830,028 C6:4-7.

52. Silberstein, D.A. Flavouring reconstituted tobacco. Tobacco Journal International, 1985. Vol.1: 26-29.

53. Method of removing nicotine from tobacco using organic solvent. Philip Morris Incorporated. Patent number 3,046,997, July 31, 1962.

54. Denicotinize tobacco by rapid drying of an alkaline aqueous dispersion of tobacco. Patent number 4,068,671. AMF Incorporated, January 17, 1978.

55. U.S. Patent No. 3,584,630. 1:57-58.

56. Leffingwell, J.C., Yound, H.J., Tobacco Flavoring for Smoking Products published by R.J. Reynolds Tobacco Co., 1972.

57. Robinson J. H. and Pritchard, W. S. The role of nicotine in tobacco use. Psychopharmacology, 1992; 108:405.

58. Rose, J.E., Levin, E.D. Inter-relationships between conditioned and primary reinforcement in the maintenance of cigarette smoking. British Journal of Addiction, 1991; 86:605-609.

59. Blanc, P. et al. Cough in hot pepper workers. Chest Vol. 99: 27, 1991.

60. Levin et al. Clinical Evaluation of a Citric Acid Inhaler for Smoking Cessation. Drug and Alcohol Dependence, 1993; 131-138.

61. Gori, G.B., Benowitz, N.L., and Lynch, C.J. Mouth versus deep airways absorption of nicotine in cigarette smokers. Pharmacology, Biochemistry & Behavior, 1986, Vol.24:1181-1184.

62. Harris, J., and Hayes, L. A method for measuring the pH value of whole smoke. Tobacco Science, 1977, Vol. XXI.

63. U.S. patent no. 4,830,028. May 16, 1989.

64. R.J. Reynolds Tobacco Company. Chemical and Biological Studies: New Cigarette Prototypes That Heat Instead of Burn Tobacco, 1988; 455-557.

65. Jenkins, R.W., Comes, R.A. Exogenous vs endogenous transfer of nicotine during smoking. The International Journal of Applied Radiation and Physics, 1976. Vol. 27:323-324.

66. Jenkins, R.W., Bass, R.T., Newell, G.C., Jr., Segura, G., Newman, R.H. Recommendations for the standardized preparation of carbon-14 labeled cigarettes. Tobacco 177(20):35-38.

67. Newsweek, March 21, 1994; 52-53, and Sunday Times of London, September 19, 1993.

68. Gelbert, D.G., Robinson, J.H., Chamberlin, C.L., Speilberger, C.D. Effects of smoking/nicotine on anxiety, heart rate, and lateralization of EEG during a stressful movie. Psychophysiology, 1989; 26(3):311-320.

69. Pritchard, W.S. Electroencephalographic effects of cigarette smoking. Psy-

chopharmacology, 1991; 104:485-490.

70. Pritchard, W.S., Duke, D.W., Coburn, K.L., Robinson, J.H. Nonlinear dynamical electroencephalographic analysis applied to nicotine psychopharmacology and Alzheimer's disease. In Lippiello, P.M., Collins, A.C., Gray, J.A., Robinson, J.H., editors. The Biology of Nicotine. New York: Raven Press, 1992; 195-214.

71. Pritchard, W.S., Duke, D.W. Modulation of EEG dimensional complexity by smoking. Journal of Psychophysiology, 1992; 6(1):1-10.

72. Pritchard, W.S., Robinson, J.H., Guy, T.D. Enhancement of continuous performance task reaction time by smoking in nondeprived smokers. Psychopharmacology, 1992; 108:437-442.

73. Pritchard, W.S., Robinson, J.H. The meaning of addiction: reply to West. Psychopharmacology, 1992; 108:411-416.

74. Robinson, J.H., Pritchard, W.S., Davis, R.A. Psychopharmacological effects of smoking a cigarette with typical "tar" and carbon monoxide yields but minimal nicotine. Psychopharmacology, 1992; 108:466-472.

75. Pritchard, W.S., Gilbert, D.G., Duke, D.W. Flexible effects of quantified cigarette-smoke delivery on EEG dimensional complexity. Psychopharmacology, 1993.

76. U.S. Patent no. 5,138,062 C4:41-48.

77. U.S. Patent no. 5,138,062 C18:1-11.

78. Pillsbury, C., Bright, K., O'Connor, J., and Irish, F.W. Tobacco: Tar and Nicotine in Cigarette Smoke. Journal of the Association of Official Analytical Chemists, 1969, Vol. 52:3:458-462.

79. Benowitz et al. Smokers of low yield cigarettes do not consume less nicotine. New England Journal of Medicine, 1983; 309:139-142.

    Benowitz, N.L. and Jacob, P. Daily intake of nicotine during cigarette smoking. Clin. Pharmacol. Ther, 1984; 35:4:499-504.

80. Benowitz et al. Smokers of low yield cigarettes do not consume less nicotine. NEJM, 1983; 309:139-142.

81. Gust and Pickens. Does cigarette nicotine yield affect puff volume? Clin. Pharmacol. Ther, 1982; 32:4:418-422.

82. Herning et al. Puff volume increase when low-nicotine cigarettes are smoked. Br. Med. J., 1981; 283:187-189.

83. Sutton et al. Relationship between cigarette yield, puffing patterns, and smoke intake: evidence for tar compensation? British Med. J., 1982; 285:600-603.

84. Wald et al. Relative intakes of tar, nicotine, and carbon monoxide from cigarettes of different yields. Thorax, 1984; 39:361-364.

85. Goldfarb et al. Reactions to cigarettes as a function of nicotine and tar. Clinical Pharmacology Ther, 1976; 19:6:767-772.

86. Maron and Fortman. Nicotine yield and measures of cigarette smoke exposure in a large population: Are lower-yield cigarettes safer? AJPH, 1987; 77:546-549.

87. Stepney, R. Consumption of cigarettes of reduced tar and nicotine delivery. British Journal of Addiction, 1980; 75:81-88.

88. Benowitz, N.L. and Jacob, P. Daily intake of nicotine during cigarette

smoking. Clin. Pharmacol. Ther, 1984; 35:4:499-504.

89. Benowitz et al. Smokers of low yield cigarettes do not consume less nicotine. NEJM, 1983; 309:139-142.

90. Kozlowski et al. The misuse of "less-hazardous" cigarettes and its detection: Hole-blocking of ventilated filters. American Journal of Public Health, 1980; Vol. 70:11:1202-03.

91. Grunberg, Neil E. et al., Changes in overwrap and butt length of American filter cigarettes. NY State J of Med, July 1985:310-12.

6

Smoking Should Not Be Regulated

Jeffrey Hart

Jeffrey Hart is a nationally syndicated columnist whose writings have appeared in the Conservative Chronicle *and the* Washington Times.

Government does not generally prohibit common behaviors on the grounds that they are harmful to people's health. But now the federal government has singled out cigarettes as politically incorrect and is trying to use their harmfulness as justification to ban smoking. Under the Constitution, the federal government has no jurisdiction over smokers. People should be allowed to make their own decision whether or not to smoke.

I know that many people say they enjoy smoking cigarettes, but I don't and never have. Still, if the current anti-smoking madness continues, I am just going to have to light up in conspicuous protest.

The fine columnist Scott McConnell writes in the *New York Post*, "The [*New York*] *Times* has found a new venue for politically correct moralizing: the obituary page. Readers were gratuitously informed that French geneticist Jerome Lejeune, dead at 67 because of lung cancer, was 'a heavy smoker.' The *Times* obit page hasn't yet begun informing us whether various people who have died of AIDS were promiscuous homosexuals, or whether heart attack victims were fat and avoided exercise—and, truth be told, we don't really expect it to. In PC land, smokers are the one social group made to feel responsible for the deleterious consequences of their own behavior."

That's right on the mark. As I understand it, living in New York City or Los Angeles and breathing the air, laden with carbon monoxide and much else, is about the same as smoking 2.5 packs of cigarettes per day.

I am not aware that any legislators, not even Rep. Henry Waxman of California, and not even Surgeon General Joycelyn Elders, are looking into banning gasoline-powered automobiles.

It is now common knowledge that fatty diets and even most red meat are bad for your arteries. I am not aware that the likes of Waxman and Elders want to outlaw red meat.

The AIDS plague is spread in two principal ways: using dirty needles

Jeffrey Hart, "Permit People to Make Their Own Decisions," *Conservative Chronicle*, May 18, 1994. Reprinted with special permission of King Features Syndicate.

and anal intercourse. Yet we can't even close the homosexual bathhouses. AIDS seems to have the standing of a chic and politically protected disease.

But the anti-smoking craze is upon us. There on the front page were seven tobacco company executives with their hands raised, taking the oath, defending themselves before the House Subcommittee on Health and Environment. The whole thing looked like a witch trial in 17th century Salem. Guilt was simply presumed.

Enormous figures were floated, e.g., that tobacco is responsible for the deaths of 400,000 people annually.

People tend to be intimidated by numbers, especially large ones, assuming that they are backed by science. But a moment's reflection will tell you that no such figure as 400,000 can possibly be substantiated by hard science. The causes of death are too multiple, and they importantly include genes. Your fate is to a great extent written in your DNA from the day you were two cells.

Smoking and the Constitution

There is the major problem here that under our Constitution the federal government, including Congress and including both Joycelyn and Hillary, has no jurisdiction whatever over the smoker. Smoking was around when the Constitution was written, and, I have to say, the document never mentions it. But the 10th Amendment does explicitly rebuff any federal move to aggrandize its power: "The powers not delegated to the United States by the Constitution, nor prohibited by it to the States, are reserved to the States respectively, or to the people."

That is clear enough. The two words "the people" mean us. Yet that Little Napoleon, Labor Secretary Bob Reich, seems to think he has the power to ban smoking in the workplace.

Look, everyone knows that smoking is not good for you. That has been known since the Indians introduced Walter Raleigh to the leaf in the 17th century. King James I, one of the most unpopular kings in British history, wrote a pamphlet against smoking, calling it sinful.

We seem to be headed back to King James' old position. Smoking is becoming a secular sin and is to be extirpated by the federal clergy.

I have several favorite pipe and cigar stores, two of them on 42nd Street in Manhattan. They both belong to an older world, a relief from the hurry hurry and chaos and carbon monoxide outdoors. It is quiet. It is male. The faint odor of various blends of tobacco is in the air. The walls are covered with pipes of all sizes and designs. The various shades and textures of wood are aesthetically fascinating. Some old pipes have come from estate sales. I myself have a pipe that was smoked by a Boer general during the Boer War. The cigars are splendid too. Some Cuban cigar makers managed to escape from Castro to the Dominican Republic, and you can still get fine Havanas. The smell if the cigars is delicious.

Of course it is outrageous that the feds continue to subsidize the tobacco growers—along with much else they should instead consign to the market.

As I said, everyone knows smoking is bad for your health. Why not let it go at that, and permit people to make their own decisions?

The market could handle it. One restaurant could put up a sign: "No Smoking." Another one could put up a "Smokers Welcome" sign. The customers would make their choice.

7

Bans on Smoking
Threaten Individual Rights

Thomas Harvey Holt

Thomas Harvey Holt is a visiting fellow at Capital Research Center and a contributor to Insight, *a weekly journal of opinion.*

Already strict limits on the number of places where smokers can go to smoke are discriminating against people who choose to smoke. Dire new warnings from the EPA about the dangers of secondhand smoke will make it easier for the government to pass comprehensive smoking bans. The American public should be wary of pronouncements about the dangers of secondhand smoke and the restrictions that will surely follow.

During the late 1890s, antismoking activists mounted a campaign against cigarettes that resulted in bans on their manufacture, sale and possession in 14 states. Many employers refused even to hire cigarette smokers. But a Senate committee, presented with a proposal for a national ban, refused to act. Only the states could enact bans, the committee said.

The modern Washington "pest class" knows no such limits. The Environmental Protection Agency with great fanfare has issued a pamphlet urging people not to smoke in their own homes, lest someone in the household be subjected to the alleged hazards of secondhand smoke. The EPA's advice is just a pesky suggestion—for now.

Smokers soon may find state social services agents on their doorsteps, demanding to know if they smoke in the presence of children. Custody battles could be decided on the basis of who smokes or who doesn't smoke. And as the Marxist Workers Vanguard has suggested, "Some job applications will read, 'Are you now, or have you ever been, a smoker?'"

Outlandish, you say? Already, discrimination against smokers is not just allowed but officially sanctioned. Smokers are relegated to huddling on curbsides like teenagers hiding behind the gym. Smoking is banned on most airline flights, buses and trains. Los Angeles has banned smoking in restaurants. And that's just cigarette smoking. Cigar and pipe smokers have been browbeaten into private dinner-and-smoke clubs. Smoking is raised increasingly as an issue in custody disputes. Tobacco advertising is banished from the airwaves, and it is under fire elsewhere.

Thomas Harvey Holt, "Pests' Attacks on Smoking Threaten Individual Freedoms," *Insight on the News*, October 18, 1993. This article first appeared in the *Washington Times*. Reprinted with permission of the *Washington Times*.

Almost all these restrictions have come about during the past 25 years, and one advocacy group has played a key role: Action on Smoking and Health, or ASH. Founded in 1967 and run by George Washington University law Professor John F. Banzhaf III, the organization has perfected the art of political litigation. It was Banzhaf's petition to the Federal Communications Commission—invoking the Fairness Doctrine to demand equal time for antismoking ads—that led to the ban on broadcast advertising for tobacco.

Given its record of success, ASH provides a glimpse of what may come. The group has filed a legal petition with the Occupational Safety and Health Administration asking for a ban on all workplace smoking. Banzhaf reportedly envisions new smoking-related definitions of child abuse and grounds for divorce (also a feature of the 19th century's anti-tobacco campaign), bans in every public place, large court awards and judicial orders forbidding smoking in private homes. ASH's newsletter notes with approval a British agency's proposal to ban adoptions by smokers.

The EPA's recent report labeling secondhand smoke (bureaucratically called environmental tobacco smoke, or ETS) a Class A carcinogen has given ASH a new line of attack.

Employing the Americans with Disabilities Act as a wedge, ASH has come out with a model complaint letter designed to scare the bejabbers out of the operators of restaurants, airports and shopping malls—almost anywhere people gather.

Discrimination against smokers is not just allowed but officially sanctioned.

The disabilities act requires that "reasonable accommodations" be provided for the handicapped, including anyone who is bothered by smoke. Complete with legal citations and references to the EPA report, the antismoking group's model complaint letter could not be more clear: Ban smoking or we'll sue.

As Banzhaf explained to *Washingtonian* magazine: Fast-food restaurants "go to great lengths to lure kids into their store. We now know from the EPA report how dangerous ETS is. You see all these little kids in the smoking section. Now what would happen if one of these kids had an asthmatic attack? The answer is pretty clear. A lawsuit could be brought on behalf of that child."

But do we really know the hazards of secondhand smoke? The EPA, in its haste to condemn tobacco, has skipped a few scientific steps, such as thorough peer review of the evidence. Studies with which the EPA disagreed—such as one by the National Cancer Institute, no tobacco industry lackey—were ignored. EPA officials simply ramrodded the secondhand smoke report through internal review processes.

According to EPA documents released at a scantily reported congressional hearing, EPA reviewers strongly questioned many of the fundamental conclusions of the report on secondhand smoke. One reviewer was especially concerned about the rather casual way in which the report links secondhand smoke and cancer and the lack of evidence to back the claim: "If you can technically show causal association, do; where you can't, don't infer it." And in reference to the agency's departure from its own scientific guidelines to label secondhand smoke a Class A carcinogen, the reviewer wrote: "Like it or not, EPA should live within its own categorization framework or clearly explain why we chose not to do so." Other reviewers expressed similar concerns.

Nonsmokers and smokers alike should be concerned about the EPA's cavalier pronouncements on secondhand smoke. If secondhand smoke is sufficient justification for the government to mount citizens' doorsteps, what other minor, politically incorrect social offenses might be the object of the pest class's next crusade? Fried foods? Alcohol, again? Or belching?

Banzhaf and his fellow activist litigators seem to have an overwhelming passion for taking the fun out of life. Unfortunately, a government that concerns itself with what people lawfully do in the privacy of their own homes seems determined to help the antifun brigade.

8

Secondhand Smoke Should Not Be Used to Justify Regulations on Smoking

Jacob Sullum

Jacob Sullum is the managing editor of Reason *magazine, a monthly journal of libertarian opinion.*

Secondhand tobacco smoke has been labeled a major health hazard by the EPA. Careful examination of the EPA's evidence reveals that they manipulated their data to arrive at a predetermined conclusion. The link between secondhand smoke and health problems is, in fact, so tenuous that it should not be used to justify further government restrictions.

"Secondhand Smoke Kills." So says a billboard on Pico Boulevard in Los Angeles that I pass every day on the way to work. I'm still not convinced. But most Americans seem to be: a CNN/*Time* poll conducted in March 1994 found that 78 per cent believe secondhand smoke is "very" or "somewhat" harmful.

That idea was endorsed by the U.S. Environmental Protection Agency in 1993, when it declared secondhand smoke "a known human lung carcinogen." Since then the EPA's report has helped justify smoking bans throughout the country: in cities such as Los Angeles and San Francisco (likely to be joined soon by New York); in Maryland, Vermont, and Washington state; and in government offices, including the Defense Department. On March 25, 1994, the Occupational Safety and Health Administration proposed a ban on smoking in workplaces, including bars and restaurants. A bill introduced by Representative Henry Waxman (D., Calif.) would go even further, banning smoking in almost every building except residences.

Most supporters of such measures probably believe that the EPA's report presents definitive scientific evidence that "secondhand smoke kills." But a closer look shows that the EPA manipulated data and finessed important points to arrive at a predetermined conclusion. The agency compromised science to support the political crusade against smoking.

The first line of defense for people who want to avoid scrutiny of the case against secondhand smoke (a/k/a environmental tobacco smoke, or ETS) is to argue by analogy. "We know that tobacco smoke causes disease and can kill you," says Scott Ballin, chairman of the Coalition on Smoking or Health. "It makes sense that a person who doesn't smoke cigarettes, who's sitting next to a smoker and inhaling the smoke, is also at some risk." The EPA offers a similar argument, devoting a chapter of its report on ETS to the evidence that smoking causes cancer.

The agency compromised science to support the political crusade against smoking.

Although superficially plausible, this analogy is misleading. A smoker breathes in hot, concentrated tobacco smoke and holds it in his lungs before exhaling. A nonsmoker in the vicinity, by contrast, breathes air that includes minute quantities of residual chemicals from tobacco smoke. "ETS is so highly diluted that it is not even appropriate to call it smoke," says Gary Huber, a professor of medicine at the University of Texas Health Science Center, writing with two colleagues in the July 1991 *Consumers' Research.* Furthermore, since many of the compounds in tobacco smoke are unstable, it is not safe to assume even that a nonsmoker is exposed to the same chemicals as a smoker. Of 50 biologically active substances thought to be present in ETS, Huber and his colleagues report, only 14 have actually been detected.

Even if exposure to ETS were analogous to smoking, the doses involved are so small that it's not clear they would have any effect. Many chemicals that are hazardous or even fatal above a certain level are harmless (or beneficial) in smaller doses. James Enstrom, a professor of epidemiology at UCLA, estimates that someone exposed to ETS would be taking in the equivalent of a few cigarettes a year, perhaps one-hundredth of a cigarette a day. Yet studies of smoking have never looked at people who smoke that little; the lowest-exposure groups have been subjects who smoke up to five cigarettes a day.

The EPA's smoking gun

So it's not reasonable to conclude that ETS must be dangerous because smoking is dangerous. You have to look at the research that deals specifically with ETS. The EPA's finding is based on 30 epidemiological studies that compared lung-cancer rates among nonsmokers (mainly women) who lived with smokers to lung-cancer rates among nonsmokers who lived with nonsmokers. None of the studies measured actual exposure to ETS; they simply assumed that people who lived with smokers were more exposed than people who didn't. In most of these studies, lung cancer was somewhat more common among the subjects living with smokers, but in only 6 cases were the results statistically significant.

This is a crucial point. In any study that compares a group exposed to a suspected risk factor with a control group, the luck of the draw may result in a difference between the two groups that does not reflect a difference between the populations the groups are supposed to represent. Researchers do statistical tests to account for the possibility of such a fluke. By convention, epidemiologists call a result significant when the probability that it occurred purely by chance is 5 per cent or less. By this standard, 80 per cent of the studies discussed by the EPA did not find a statistically significant link between ETS and lung cancer.

But the EPA, which had always used the conventional definition of statistical significance in its risk assessments, adopted a different standard for the report on ETS. It considered a result significant if the probability that it occurred purely by chance was 10 per cent or less. This change essentially doubles the odds of being wrong. "The justification for this usage," according to the report itself, "is based on the *a priori* hypothesis . . . that a positive association exists between exposure to ETS and lung cancer." Of course, the EPA was supposed to test that hypothesis, not simply assume that it is true.

Instead of presenting results from the epidemiological studies as they originally appeared, the EPA recalculated them using the less rigorous standard. As a report from the Congressional Research Service dryly notes, "it is unusual to return to a study after the fact, lower the required significance level, and declare its results to be supportive rather than unsupportive of the effect one's theory suggests should be present."

Even after the EPA massaged the data, the vast majority of the studies still did not show a significant association between ETS and lung cancer. Of the 11 U.S. studies, only 1 yielded a result that was significant according to the looser definition. (According to the usual definition, none of them did.) To bolster the evidence, the EPA did a "meta-analysis" of these studies. Dr. Enstrom notes that this technique was originally intended for clinical trials that assess the impact of a drug or procedure by randomly assigning subjects to treatment and control groups. By contrast, the data analyzed by the EPA came from retrospective case-control studies that "matched" people with lung cancer to people without lung cancer. Enstrom says using meta-analysis for such studies "is not a particularly meaningful exercise," because the studies are apt to differ in the way they define exposure, the confounding variables they take into account, the types of cancer they include, and so on.

In any event, the EPA's conclusion—that living with a smoker raises a woman's risk of getting lung cancer by 19 per cent—is justified only according to the definition of statistical significance adopted especially for these data. By the usual standard, even the meta-analysis does not support the claim that ETS causes lung cancer. Furthermore, the EPA excluded from its analysis a major U.S. study, published in the November 1992 *American Journal of Public Health*, that failed to find a significant link between ETS and lung cancer. Given the large size of the study, it could well have changed the outcome of the meta-analysis, so that the result would not have been significant even by the EPA's revised standard.

Small claims

Despite this "fancy statistical footwork," as a July 1992 article in *Science* described it, the EPA was able to claim only a weak association between ETS and lung cancer. With a risk increase as low as 19 per cent, it is difficult to rule out the possibility that other factors were at work. "At least 20 confounding variables have been identified as important to the development of lung cancer," write Huber et al. "No reported study comes anywhere close to controlling, or even mentioning, half of these."

Smokers tend to differ from nonsmokers in many ways—including diet, socioeconomic status, risk-taking behavior, and exercise—and it is likely that the spouses of smokers share these characteristics to some extent. "If wives of smokers share in poor health habits or other factors that could contribute to illness," the Congressional Research Service notes, "statistical associations found between disease and passive smoking could be incidental or misleading."

Misclassification could also account for some or all of the observed differences between wives of smokers and wives of nonsmokers. It's possible that some of the subjects thought to be nonsmokers were actually smokers or former smokers. Since spouses of smokers are more likely to be smokers themselves, such errors would have biased the results. The EPA adjusted the data to account for this effect, but it's impossible to say whether it fully compensated for misclassification.

Even if exposure to ETS [environmental tobacco smoke] were analogous to smoking, the doses involved are so small that it's not clear they would have any effect.

These issues are especially important when the relationship between a suspected risk factor and a disease is weak. Based on the 11 U.S. studies, the EPA concluded that a woman who lives with a smoker is 1.19 times as likely to get lung cancer as a woman who lives with a nonsmoker. This ratio did not rise above 2.1 to 1 in any of the U.S. studies. In previous risk assessments, the EPA has seen such weak associations as cause for skepticism. When the agency examined the alleged connection between electromagnetic fields and cancer, for example, it said, "the association is not strong enough to constitute a proven causal relationship, largely because the relative risks in the published reports have seldom exceeded 3.0."

This concern did not prevent the EPA from reaching a firm conclusion about ETS, even though the agency recognized the limitations of the data. The head of the Scientific Advisory Board that reviewed the report conceded: "This is a classic case where the evidence is not all that strong."

The evidence is especially unimpressive when compared to the evidence that smoking causes lung cancer. In the latter case, there are thousands of studies, and virtually all of them have found a positive association, statistically significant in the vast majority of cases. And the associations are sizable: a typical female smoker is about 10 times as likely to get lung cancer as a female nonsmoker; for men the ratio is more like 20 to 1; and among heavy smokers, the figures are even higher. "The data on active smoking are so much stronger," Enstrom says. "That should be the focus of attention, not something which is so small and has the potential to be confounded by so many different things. I personally am baffled as to why people give it so much credibility."

Protected from themselves

The explanation may be that the EPA's conclusion about ETS is useful in a way that the evidence about smoking is not. Although the share of adults who smoke has dropped from about 40 per cent to about 25 per cent since 1965, some 50 million Americans continue to smoke. And as

Duke University economist W. Kip Viscusi shows in his recent book *Smoking: Making the Risky Decision*, this is not because they are ignorant about the health effects. Rather, they are willing to accept the risks in exchange for the benefits of smoking. From a "public-health" perspective, this is intolerable; no one should be allowed to make such a foolish decision. But the idea of protecting people from themselves still arouses considerable opposition in this country. Hence anti-smoking activists and public-health officials need a different excuse for restricting smoking: it endangers innocent bystanders.

When EPA Administrator Carol Browner testified in favor of Waxman's Smoke-Free Environment Act [a bill to ban smoking in nonresidential buildings] in February 1994, she relied heavily on the ETS report. But the main benefit that she claimed for the bill was its expected impact on smokers. "The reduction in smoker mortality due to smokers who quit, cut back, or do not start is estimated to range from about 33,000 to 99,000 lives per year," she said. And six surgeons general, reported the *New York Times*, "echoed the theme that this simple measure could do more for the public health than any other bill in years."

If your main goal is improving "the public health," you may be inclined to shade the truth a bit if it helps to make smoking less acceptable and more inconvenient. Marc Lalonde, Canada's former minister of national health and welfare, offered a rationale for such a strategy in a highly influential 1974 report: "Science is full of 'ifs,' 'buts,' and 'maybes,' while messages designed to influence the public must be loud, clear, and unequivocal. . . . The scientific 'yes, but' is essential to research, but for modifying human behavior of the population it sometimes produces the 'uncertain sound.' This is all the excuse needed by many to cultivate and tolerate an environment and lifestyle that is hazardous to health."

Writing about the ETS controversy in *Toxicologic Pathology*, Yale University epidemiologist Alvan Feinstein quotes a colleague who appears to have been influenced by the Lalonde Doctrine: "Yes, it's rotten science, but it's in a worthy cause. It will help us get rid of cigarettes and become a smoke-free society."

This seems to be the attitude that the EPA brought to its risk assessment. In June 1990 the agency released the first draft of *Environmental Tobacco Smoke: A Guide to Workplace Smoking Policies*, intended to advise employers to institute smoking restrictions. Yet this was three and a half years before the EPA officially determined that ETS was a health hazard. In a letter to Representative Thomas J. Bliley Jr. (R., Va.), then EPA Administrator William Reilly admitted that "beginning the development of an Agency risk assessment after the commencement of work on the draft policy guide gave the appearance of the very situation—i.e., policy leading science—that I am committed to avoid."

Reilly was so committed to avoiding this appearance that he decided not to release the final version of the policy guide, even though it was ready by December 1992. As he explained to the *Wall Street Journal*, putting out the guide along with the risk assessment would "look like we're trying to torque the science." But don't worry. Miss Browner, Mr. Reilly's successor, released the handy pamphlet in July 1993.

9

Cigarette Tax Increases Would Be Harmful

Brian Robertson

Brian Robertson is a contributing editor at Insight, *a weekly journal of opinion.*

In 1993, the Clinton Administration proposed a large tax increase on cigarettes to help finance its national health care plan. Such a tax increase would harm the economy by severely damaging the tobacco industry: costing jobs, decreasing income tax revenues, and reducing the consumption of goods and services. Black market activities, especially smuggling along the Mexican border, would also increase in response to the demand for cheaper cigarettes.

When Hillary Rodham Clinton banned smoking in the White House, America's struggling tobacco farmers knew they were in a for a rough four years. In September 1993, they found out just how rough.

The Clinton administration's plan to overhaul the nation's health care system includes a hefty new excise tax on tobacco—an increase of between 75 cents and $1 from the current 24 cents per pack of cigarettes—as part of its financing. While this unprecedented increase has won applause from the influential anti-smoking lobby, opponents warn that a tax of this magnitude could devastate an industry vital to the Southeast and give rise to a level of black market activity that hasn't been seen since Prohibition. These critics believe that the administration is taking an enormous economic and social risk in a misguided effort at deficit financing and social engineering.

It was clear from Mrs. Clinton's comments before the House Ways and Means Committee that there is more to the proposed tax than "revenue enhancement." Reporters and legislators alike had high praise for the first lady's eloquence and political dexterity—she even elicited an ovation from jaded congressmen—but Republican Rep. Jim Bunning of Kentucky appeared less impressed than his colleagues. When, on September 28, Bunning asked her why tobacco was being singled out while other potentially harmful substances, such as sugar and alcohol, were spared, she evaded the question, replying that there was "no free lunch in this pro-

Brian Robertson, "Tobacco Tax Plan Lights Up Controversy," *Insight on the News*, November 8, 1993. Reprinted with permission.

gram" and insisting that "everybody is going to pay." She added point-
edly, "If there is a way that you can ever come up with to tax the substances like the ones you've just named, we'll be glad to look at it."

But Mrs. Clinton already had answered the congressman's question
during the previous day's testimony. "Tobacco is the only product that,
if used as directed, can have such damaging health consequences," she
said. "Neither alcohol nor caffeine nor the others, if used in moderation
or in small amounts, are proven to have the same kind of effects."

Destroying the tobacco industry

That kind of talk scares North Carolinians. "I can't go along with any argument when it means destroying an entire industry," says Pender Sharp,
a tobacco farmer in Sims. "A $1 increase in cigarette taxes would proba-
bly put half the tobacco farmers in this area out of business, and that's
only a small minority of the people that would lose their jobs."

According to Sharp, the income produced by tobacco farming and
cigarette manufacturing is regenerated throughout the state economy.
"We operate an average-size farm, and we put about $1 million each year
into the local economy in the form of wages and buying goods and services to operate the business," he says. "If we go down, that takes a big
slug of money out of the economy." Many industry studies have reached
the same conclusion, estimating that a $1-a-pack increase in the cigarette
tax would mean a 17 percent decline in cigarette sales and a loss of close
to 400,000 jobs, more than 100,000 in the tobacco industry alone.

Those kinds of forecasts in turn scare lawmakers who represent
tobacco-growing areas. "Singling out tobacco for tax increases of this
magnitude will do more damage to the economy in the Southeast U.S.
than Sherman's march to the sea," argues Bunning. Sources on Capitol
Hill acknowledge that a vote for any tax higher than 25 cents a pack
would be political suicide for those whose districts depend on tobacco.

"I guess it comes down to how much they need our vote for the
health care bill," says North Carolina Democratic Rep. Tim Valentine. If
the vote is close, as it was on the president's budget, the administration
might have to negotiate. "The White House learned a lesson worth four
years in college when they lost the vote on the economic stimulus package," says Valentine. "That time they sent it up to the Hill with the in-
structions 'Don't touch it!' and it went down in flames. This time they
might be a little more open to changes."

---

*A $1 increase in cigarette taxes would probably put
half the tobacco farmers in this area out of business.*

The budget vote itself underscores how much the administration
needs the tobacco vote. An obscure provision of that bill required that 75
percent of the tobacco used to make cigarettes in the United States be
grown domestically, effectively limiting the import of cheaper, foreign-
grown varieties increasingly favored by domestic manufacturers. Despite
denials from all parties that this "domestic content" legislation was included by the administration to secure the tobacco bloc, some find it
more than coincidental that, when the budget passed by just one vote in
both the House and Senate, 30 out of 34 House Democrats from tobacco

districts voted in its favor.

The administration may be less willing to negotiate on the tobacco levy. Congress already has expressed deep concern about the package's [health care] financing, and the president is counting on the new tax to generate $17 billion a year to cover costs. Unlike other possible taxes, a higher tax on tobacco products has widespread support among the three out of four Americans who don't smoke, as well as powerful backing from anti-smoking lobbyists, who already have won major tax battles in states such as New York and California. And because lighting up is increasingly regarded as an antisocial activity, tobacco is a much easier target for a "sin" tax than alcohol. Also, the impact of a tobacco tax would be felt mainly in the Southeast (although convenience stores nationwide make up to one-fourth of their income from tobacco sales) whereas a stiff new tax on alcohol would be felt by a range of businesses all over the country.

Some tobacco tax proponents feel that an increase of 75 cents or $1 a pack doesn't go far enough, being too low to have a serious effect on consumption. Former Surgeon General C. Everett Koop recently joined the ranks of these critics in a *Washington Post* op-ed piece that suggested a stiffer increase. Even tobacco farmers would benefit from a $2-a-pack tax, wrote Koop. "Most tobacco farmers know the right and smart thing to do is to get out of a business that produces disease, disability and death, and this tax can help them make the transition to the smoke-free society and smoke-free economy that lie in our future. A small percentage of the revenue from this tax could be returned to tobacco-growing states to be used to help tobacco farmers diversify. . . . Tobacco-state members of Congress should be fighting for their share of the pie to help move their states into the economy of the 21st century." The White House plan includes just such a subsidy to help farmers convert to other crops.

Sharp thinks that those who suggest the mass conversion of crops simply don't know what they're talking about. "We hear people all the time outside the industry saying, 'Why not grow another crop?' Well, it's because we can't financially. . . . An acre of corn might make $15 or $20 an acre in net profit, while a tobacco crop will consistently make $800 to $1,000 an acre in net profit."

Moreover, converting from one crop to another involves more than digging up and replacing plants. "Farming's a pretty big business," says Sharp, "and most farms that you see today have about $1 million to $5 million invested in equipment and property, and they operate like any other small business—with pretty good-size payrolls, lots of government regulations and red tape to deal with—and are very vulnerable to a drastic change in the market." Tobacco farmers on the whole complain that the government's attitude of "let them grow soybeans" shows indifference to the realities of their situation.

Encouraging tobacco growing

Ironically, Washington's policies since the New Deal have encouraged farmers to grow tobacco. Begun to help lift farmers out of the Depression, government subsidy programs set limits on the acreage tobacco farmers could plant, then guaranteed the price they got for their crops. After World War II, farmers created cooperatives to administer the program, buy up crops that were not sold and set the acreage allotments. The government continued to set the price floor and provide loans to the cooperatives until the early 1980s, when the cooperatives imposed annual assessments on tobacco farmers to build up reserves.

Today the government limits its role to low-interest loans, and the farmers insist—with some justification—that subsidies are a thing of the past. But it is true that the size and profitability of the industry can be traced to Washington's intervention.

Aside from questions of fairness, the administration's twin goals of reducing smoking while boosting revenue may be an exercise in frustration. Critics point to the experience of Canada to show the unpredictability of such efforts. Between 1984 and 1992, federal and provincial governments there raised the excise tax on tobacco by more than 200 percent. While Canada asserts that cigarette consumption is down by 38 percent and that revenues have increased by $2.5 billion ($1.87 billion U.S.), those figures don't tell the whole story.

Duty-free sales and exports have risen almost tenfold during the same period, and studies show that one in six packs of cigarettes consumed in Canada in 1992 was contraband. If these smuggled cigarettes are factored in, according to one widely quoted study, "it appears fiscal policy has proved ineffective in reducing the consumption of tobacco."

Singling out tobacco for tax increases . . . will do more damage to the economy in the Southeast U.S. than Sherman's march to the sea.

With the most recent steep increase in Canada's federal tax on tobacco, in 1992, the government found that it yielded less than two-thirds of the revenue forecast; the rest was swallowed up by the growing black market. The government in Ottawa, relying on tobacco taxes to fight its deficits, has cracked down on black market sales, but with little success. The financial incentives for those involved in the illegal trade are too great, and government resources for enforcement too limited. Cigarette-related crimes have soared, including robberies and hijackings. In September 1993 there was an attempt on the life of the mayor of Cornwall, Ontario, who had tried to shut off the flow through his border city.

A troubling by-product of Canada's tobacco tax has been the creation of a criminal subculture among Canadian Indians who live near the border. Because Indian reservations are, by law, semiautonomous, there is little that customs officials can do to stem the flow of duty-free cigarettes from the U.S. into Canada through this route. Canadian smokers pour into the reservations seeking cheap smokes, many reselling them for a profit on the streets.

Most Canadians wink at cigarette smugglers as Americans winked at bootleggers in the 1920s, but the illicit trade has divided the Indian community. Radical separatists are using the trade to consolidate political power and so gain complete autonomy in order to evade customs, and are using the money to stockpile weapons. Others, meanwhile, are concerned about the corrupting effect the traffic in illegal tobacco has on the community.

While few foresee that level of black market activity in the United States, some believe a $1-per-pack increase in the U.S. tobacco tax would inevitably increase smuggling along the Mexican border. "We've already noticed an increase in illegal activity in California as a result of our [state] tax increase," says Monte Williams, an administrator in the excise taxes division of the California State Board of Equalization. "We went from 10 to 35 cents a pack back in January of '89, and we've had a large increase in felony and misdemeanor convictions for smuggling since then." He says the "potential's definitely there" for an explosion of black market activity and speculates that it wouldn't be in border states only. "Once you get it across the border, if you're organized at all, to get it between the states wouldn't be anywhere near as difficult."

10

Regulating Nicotine as a Drug Is Unnecessary

William I. Campbell

William I. Campbell is the president and chief executive officer of Philip Morris U.S.A., one of the nation's largest tobacco companies.

Cigarettes are not addictive. People smoke because they enjoy doing so. Charges that the tobacco industry has been altering the nicotine level of cigarettes in order to keep their customers addicted are false. The Food and Drug Administration, therefore, has no cause to regulate nicotine as a drug.

I would like to take this opportunity to set the record straight on charges that have recently been made against the [tobacco] industry and Philip Morris. First, Philip Morris does not add nicotine to our cigarettes. Second, Philip Morris does not "manipulate" or independently "control" the level of nicotine in our products. Third, Philip Morris has not used patented processes to increase or maintain nicotine levels. Fourth, cigarette smoking is not addictive. Fifth, Philip Morris has not hidden research which says that it is. And, finally, consumers are not misled by the published nicotine deliveries as measured by the FTC [Federal Trade Commission] method.

I trust that you are sincerely interested in learning the facts about the various issues raised March 25, 1994, in Food and Drug Administration (FDA) Commissioner David Kessler's presentation—issues which, I might add, are not new. The claim that cigarette smoking is addictive has been made for many years. The fact that tar and nicotine levels vary among our many products has been publicized for over 20 years. The process by which cigarettes are manufactured, and which, at our invitation, FDA representatives saw firsthand, has been publicly known for over 50 years. And the call for the FDA to assert, or be given, jurisdiction over cigarettes has been made and rejected by the FDA and the courts on several occasions in the past.

There were a number of incorrect statements or assumptions in Dr. Kessler's presentation. Many require a detailed rebuttal. I will try to respond to them.

The claim that Philip Morris secretly adds nicotine during the manu-

Testimony of William I. Campbell before the U.S. House of Representatives Committee on Energy and Commerce, Subcommittee on Health and the Environment, April 14, 1994.

facturing process to "keep smokers addicted" is a false and irresponsible charge. The processes used to manufacture cigarettes have been publicly disclosed for years in patents and the published literature. And the results of that processing—cigarettes with varying levels of tar and nicotine reflecting varying customer preferences—have been closely monitored and reported by the FTC, and the manufacturers themselves in every advertisement, for 25 years.

Contrary to the claim that we are committed to maintaining, or even increasing, nicotine delivery in our products, the fact is that tar *and nicotine* levels have decreased dramatically over the past 40 years. Today, the market is populated with a number of "ultra low" brands which deliver less than 5% of the tar *and nicotine* of popular brands 20 years ago.

Philip Morris and other manufacturers have reduced delivery in a number of ways. The most important is the use of increasingly efficient filters which substantially *reduce* many smoke components, including both tar *and nicotine*. Filtration reduces nicotine delivery 35% to 45% in today's brands, as compared to a "standard" cigarette made simply of tobacco and paper.

Through a process called ventilation, nicotine levels are reduced by 10% to 50%. Through the use of expanded tobacco—a process developed by Philip Morris, in which tobacco is "puffed" much like puffed rice cereal—tar and nicotine levels are reduced still further.

Cigarette smoking is not addictive.

There has been a fair amount of recent discussion of the reconstituted tobacco process. Again, that process has been thoroughly described for years in the published literature. In that process, stems and small leaf parts are re-formed into a paper-like sheet. The reconstituted leaf process does *not* increase nicotine levels in tobacco or cigarettes. *To the contrary, 20% to 25% of the nicotine in the tobacco used to make reconstituted leaf is lost and not replaced.*

These processes, when combined in the cigarettes Philip Morris sells today, *reduce* nicotine delivery levels by more than 50% in the case of Marlboro, to 96% in the case of Merit Ultima, as compared to a "standard" cigarette made of nothing but tobacco and paper.

Ignoring these reductions, some critics have focused on minute amounts of nicotine that are found in tobacco extracts and denatured alcohol—which *together* have no measurable effect on nicotine delivery of our cigarettes.

Philip Morris uses denatured alcohol to spray flavors on the tobacco. The alcohol is denatured—that is, it is made to taste bitter so that no one will drink it—*under a formula required by the BATF [Bureau of Alcohol, Tobacco, and Firearms] and found in the Federal Register.*

Again, the small amount of nicotine found in denatured alcohol and tobacco extracts cannot be measured in cigarette smoke.

The expenditure of millions of dollars to reduce tar and nicotine in these various ways undercuts any suggestion that Philip Morris is "intent" on adding nicotine to its cigarettes in an effort to "maintain" nicotine levels or to "addict" smokers.

The cigarette industry markets and advertises products by tar category to satisfy a variety of consumer preferences. Within tar categories, we attempt to provide a competitive advantage by providing the best possible taste.

When creating a cigarette for a tar category, we select a particular tobacco blend and flavors to provide "uniqueness" for the product. The most significant parameters for determining tar delivery are the amount of expanded tobacco used, filtration efficiency, and ventilation.

So, how do we "manipulate" or independently "control" nicotine as our critics charge? *The answer is we don't.* We accept the nicotine levels that result from this process.

As representatives of the FDA learned when, at our invitation, they recently visited our manufacturing center in Richmond, Virginia, nicotine levels in tobacco are measured at only two points in the manufacturing process—at the stemmery, where tobacco leaves are prepared for processing, and then *18 months later* after those leaves have been manufactured into finished cigarettes. Although Philip Morris maintains over 400 quality control checkpoints in the manufacturing process—for example, moisture levels, weight, etc.—*none* measures, reports or analyzes nicotine levels in tobacco.

No secret patents are used

Commissioner Kessler spent a great deal of his recent testimony attempting to support the proposition that Philip Morris may be using secret patented processes to increase or maintain nicotine delivery in our cigarettes. We are not.

The processes described in the patents referred to by Commissioner Kessler are not at all secret but, rather, were publicly disclosed years ago, first to the U.S. government and then to the world.

Philip Morris in fact has never used any of the processes described in these patents to increase, or even maintain, nicotine levels in any of its products. To the contrary, the only patents cited by Commissioner Kessler which Philip Morris has ever used were for the *reduction* and in some cases the virtual *elimination* of nicotine.

Cigarette smoking is not addictive

During the March 25 hearing, Dr. Kessler and some Members of the Subcommittee contended that nicotine is an addictive drug and that, therefore, smokers are drug addicts. I object to the premise and to the conclusion.

Many people like to smoke. Some people like the look and feel of the pack or the smell of tobacco. Some like to hold and fiddle with a cigarette. And, of course, there is the taste and aroma of the tobacco, and the sight of the smoke.

Cigarettes contain nicotine because it occurs naturally in tobacco. Nicotine contributes to the taste of cigarettes and the pleasure of smoking. The presence of nicotine, however, does not make cigarettes a drug or smoking an addiction.

People can and do quit smoking. According to the 1988 Surgeon General's Report, there are over 40 million former smokers in the United States, and 90% of smokers quit on their own, without any outside help.

Further, smoking is not intoxicating. No one gets drunk from cigarettes, and no one has said that smokers cannot function normally. Smoking does not impair judgment. No one is likely to be arrested for driving under the influence of cigarettes.

In short, our customers enjoy smoking for many reasons. Smokers are not drug addicts.

At the March 25 hearing, Commissioner Kessler repeated the charges of Dr. Jack Henningfield, that in 1983, a company, later publicly identified as Philip Morris, suppressed research by one of its scientists which allegedly concluded that nicotine was an addictive substance. That claim is false.

Tar and nicotine *levels have decreased dramatically over the past 40 years.*

In fact, that scientist published two full papers and five abstracts concerning the work in question *prior* to the creation of the manuscript in question. That manuscript did present some evidence that nicotine will be self-administered by rats and is, therefore, a "weak" reinforcing agent. But the manuscript itself states

> that termination of prolonged access to nicotine under conditions in which it functions as a positive reinforcer does not result in physiological dependence.

The manuscript thus did not conclude that nicotine is "addictive."

Moreover, by the time the Philip Morris researcher was ready to publish this information (1983), the "positive reinforcing" nature of nicotine had already been reported in other *published* literature. Indeed, the 1988 Surgeon General's Report states that such nicotine reinforcement was "shown conclusively" as early as *1981*, based on *government*-supported research.

Consumers are not misled

Contrary to the impression given by Commissioner Kessler that the FTC has somehow adopted a test procedure that misleads the public as to the true levels of tar and nicotine they are inhaling, the routine Analytical Smoking Methods derived from the FTC method are nearly identical to those used throughout the world to measure tar and nicotine deliveries and accurately compare brand deliveries.

All of the tests are conducted on cigarettes obtained from the marketplace. They are, therefore, the same cigarettes smoked by the consumer after all cigarette manufacturing processes have been completed.

As a result of this testing, the nicotine delivery of all commercial cigarettes is measured and disclosed to the tenth of a milligram, both in public releases by the FTC and, perhaps more importantly, *in every cigarette advertisement.*

Commissioner Kessler suggested that the FTC figures were misleading because smokers might "compensate" for lower tar and lower nicotine brands by smoking those cigarettes differently. In fact, the data indicates that, despite the dramatic reductions in tar and nicotine levels over the past decades, the number of cigarettes smoked by an individual has remained constant, and even declined slightly. More importantly, the data shows no difference in the number of cigarettes smoked by those who favor higher and lower yield brands.

An agency of the U.S. government charged with protecting the health of the public against impure and unsafe foods, drugs, cosmetics, and other potential hazards, the FDA has sought the regulation of nicotine as a drug and has investigated manipulation of nicotine levels in cigarettes by the tobacco industry. It provides copies of congressional testimony given in the debate over regulation of nicotine.

Foundation for Economic Education
30 S. Broadway
Irvington-on-Hudson, NY 10533
(914) 591-7230

This nonpolitical educational group promotes private property, the free market, and limited government. Its monthly journal *The Freeman* has published articles opposing regulation of the tobacco industry.

Group Against Smokers' Pollution (GASP)
PO Box 632
College Park, MD 20741-0632
(301) 459-4791

GASP works to promote the rights of nonsmokers, to educate the public about the dangers of secondhand smoke, and to regulate smoking in public places. It supports laws designed to reduce environmental tobacco smoke. The group publishes a quarterly newsletter, provides information about secondhand smoke and smoking laws, and distributes signs, buttons, and stickers.

Libertarian Party
1528 Pennsylvania Ave. SE
Washington, DC 20003
(202) 543-1988

The goal of this political party is to ensure respect for individual rights. It opposes regulation of smoking. The party publishes the bimonthly *Libertarian Party News* and periodic *Issue Papers*.

National Restaurant Association
Dept. of Technical Services
1200 17th St. NW
Washington, DC 20036
(800) 424-5156, ext. 5375

The association is the leading trade group for the food service industry, with twenty-five thousand members representing 150,000 food service outlets. Opposing government bans on or regulation of smoking in restaurants, it favors allowing each individual restaurant to set its own smoking policy. It provides written analyses of pending legislation on government regulations affecting the restaurant industry and publishes the book *Smoking in Restaurants: A Consumer Attitude Survey* as well as several newsletters.

Reason Foundation
3415 S. Sepulveda Blvd., Suite 400
Los Angeles, CA 90034
(310) 391-2245

The Reason Foundation is a libertarian research and education foundation that works to promote free markets and limited government. It publishes the monthly *Reason* magazine, which occasionally contains articles opposing the regulation of smoking.

SmokeFree Educational Services, Inc.
375 South End Ave., Suite 32F
New York, NY 10280
(212) 912-0960

This organization works to educate youth on the relationship between smoking and health. It publishes the quarterly newsletter *SmokeFree Air* and the book *Kids Say Don't Smoke* and distributes posters, stickers, and videotapes.

Smoker's Rights Alliance
20 E. Main St., Suite 710
Mesa, AZ 85201
(602) 461-8882

The alliance challenges antismoking legislation and discrimination against smokers. It believes that disputes about smoking should be settled by individuals, not by government regulations prohibiting smoking. It publishes *Smoke Signals* quarterly.

Smoking Policy Institute
218 Broadway
Seattle, WA 98102
(206) 324-4444

The institute assists companies in solving the problems created by smoking at work. It helps companies develop and implement customized smoking control policies through information packages and consulting services. The institute maintains a resource center of articles and statistics on smoking, and it publishes booklets and videotapes on workplace smoking.

The Tobacco Institute
1875 I St., NW
Washington, DC 20006
(202) 457-4800

The institute is the primary national lobbying organization for the tobacco industry. The institute argues that the dangers of smoking have not been proven and opposes regulation of tobacco. It provides the public with general information on smoking issues.

Tobacco Products Liability Project (TPLP)
Tobacco Control Resource Center
Northeastern University School of Law
400 Huntington Ave.
Boston, MA 02115-5098
(617) 373-2026

Founded in 1984 by doctors, academics, and attorneys, TPLP studies, encourages, and coordinates product liability suits in order to publicize the effects of smoking on health. It publishes the monthly newsletter *Tobacco on Trial*.

Bibliography

Books

Steve Allen	*The Passionate Nonsmokers' Bill of Rights.* New York: William Morrow, 1989.
John C. Burnham	*Bad Habits: Drinking, Smoking, Taking Drugs, Sexual Misbehavior, and Swearing in America.* New York: New York University Press, 1993.
Don Cahalan	*An Ounce of Prevention: Strategies for Solving Tobacco, Alcohol and Drug Problems.* San Francisco: Jossey-Bass, 1991.
Frank Chaloupka	*Men, Women, and Addiction: The Case of Cigarette Smoking.* Cambridge, MA: National Bureau of Economic Research, 1990.
Claire Chollat-Traquet	*Women and Tobacco.* Geneva: World Health Organization, 1992.
Judith A. Douville	*Active and Passive Smoking Hazards in the Workplace.* New York: Van Nostrand Reinhold, 1990.
Robert Goodin	*No Smoking: The Ethical Issues.* Chicago: University of Chicago Press, 1989.
Jordan Goodman	*Tobacco in History.* New York: Routledge, 1993.
Peter D. Jacobson	*The Political Evolution of Anti-Smoking Legislation.* Santa Monica, CA: RAND Corp., 1992.
Richard Klein	*Cigarettes Are Sublime.* Durham, NC: Duke University Press, 1994.
David Krogh	*Smoking: The Artificial Passion.* New York: W.H. Freeman, 1991.
Stanton Peele	*Diseasing of America: Addiction Treatment Out of Control.* Lexington, MA: Lexington Books, 1989.
Robert L. Rabin and Stephen D. Sugarman	*Smoking Policy: Law, Politics, and Culture.* New York: Oxford University Press, 1993.
William A. Timmins	*Smoking and the Workplace.* New York: Quorum Books, 1989.
W. Kip Viscusi	*Smoking: Making the Risky Decision.* New York: Oxford University Press, 1993.

Periodicals

Robert J. Barro	"Send Regulations Up in Smoke," *The Wall Street Journal,* June 3, 1994.
Carl E. Bartecchi, Thomas D. MacKenzie, and Robert W. Schrier	"The Human Costs of Tobacco Use," Part 1, *The New England Journal of Medicine,* March 31, 1994.
Peter L. Berger	"Furtive Smokers—and What They Tell Us About America," *Commentary,* June 1994.

74

William Booth — "In North Carolina, a Way of Life Is Wilting," *The Washington Post National Weekly Edition*, June 13-19, 1994.

Dennis L. Breo — "Kicking Butts—AMA, Joe Camel, and the 'Black Flag' War on Tobacco," *JAMA*, October 27, 1993.

Peter Brimelow — "Thank You for Smoking . . . ?" *Forbes*, July 4, 1994.

Shannon Brownlee — "The Smoke Next Door," *U.S. News & World Report*, June 20, 1994.

Joseph A. Califano — "If Only We'd Known," *The Washington Post National Weekly Edition*, June 6-12, 1994.

Justin Catanoso — "Butt Out," *The Washington Monthly*, January/February 1993.

Mona Charen — "Congressmen Know They Can't Ban Cigarettes," *Conservative Chronicle*, May 4, 1994. Available from PO Box 11297, Des Moines, IA 50340-1297.

Congressional Digest — "Second-Hand Tobacco Smoke," whole issue of congressional testimony, May 1994. Available from the Congressional Digest Corp., 3231 P St. NW, Washington, DC 20007.

Clifford E. Douglas — "The Tobacco Industry's Use of Nicotine as a Drug," *Priorities*, vol. 6, no. 2, 1994. Available from the American Council on Science and Health, 1995 Broadway, 2nd Fl., New York, NY 10023-5860.

Steven B. Duke and Albert C. Gross — "Regulate Tobacco, Regulate All Drugs," *The New York Times*, July 24, 1994.

Nicholas Eberstadt — "Are Smokers Rational?" *The Public Interest*, Spring 1993.

Alix M. Freedman and Laurie P. Cohen — "Smoke and Mirrors," *The Wall Street Journal*, February 11, 1993.

Ellen Goodman — "New Smokescreen for Tobacco Industry," *Liberal Opinion Week*, July 11, 1994. Available from 108 E. Fifth St., Vinton, IA 52349.

Jane Gravelle and Dennis Zimmerman — "Up in Smoke: Arguments for a Higher Tax on Cigarettes Should Be Filtered Through Fairness," *The Washington Post National Weekly Edition*, June 13-19, 1994.

Bob Herbert — "Cigarette Smoke and Mirrors," *The New York Times*, March 9, 1994.

Philip J. Hilts — "Cigarette Makers Debated the Risks They Denied," *The New York Times*, June 16, 1994.

Philip J. Hilts — "Cigarette Makers Dispute Reports on Addictiveness," *The New York Times*, April 15, 1994.

Linda Himelstein et al. — "Tobacco: Does It Have a Future?" *Business Week*, July 4, 1994.

Alice Horrigan — "The Smoking Gun," *E*, September/October 1994.

Gary L. Huber, Robert E. Brockie, and Vijay K. Mahajan — "Smoke and Mirrors: The EPA's Flawed Study of Environmental Tobacco Smoke and Lung Cancer," *Regulation*, no. 3, 1993. Available from the Cato Institute, 1000 Massachusetts Ave. NW, Washington, DC 20001.

James J. Kilpatrick   "Does Constitution Protect a 'Right to Smoke?'" *Conservative Chronicle*, March 30, 1994.

Myron Levin   "Who's Behind the Building Doctor?" *The Nation*, August 9-16, 1993.

National Review   "Second-Hand Science," July 19, 1993.

The New Yorker   "Blowing Smoke," June 13, 1994.

Anna Quindlen   "Second-Stage Smoke," *The New York Times*, April 30, 1994.

Anna Quindlen   "The Smoke Bomb," *The New York Times*, January 15, 1994.

James Ridgeway   "Where There's Smoke: The Tobacco Industry Fights Back," *The Village Voice*, November 9, 1993.

Roger Rosenblatt   "How Tobacco Executives Live with Themselves," *Business and Society Review*, Spring 1994.

Carl Rowan   "What Do We Do About Cigarettes?" *Liberal Opinion Week*, July 11, 1994.

Carl Rowan   "When the 'Rights' of Smokers and Non-Smokers Conflict," *Liberal Opinion Week*, January 18, 1993.

Hobart Rowen   "The Battle Against Tobacco," *Liberal Opinion Week*, June 20, 1994.

Terry A. Rustin   "Death and Disease for Sale," *Priorities*, Winter 1993.

David Satcher and Michael Eriksen   "The Paradox of Tobacco Control," *JAMA*, February 23, 1994.

John Schwartz   "'David's Time Against Goliath Has Come,'" *The Washington Post National Weekly Edition*, May 23-29, 1994.

John Schwartz   "The FDA Sets Its Sights on Policing Nicotine," *The Washington Post National Weekly Edition*, June 27-July 3, 1994.

John Schwartz   "Smoking Under Siege," *The Washington Post National Weekly Edition*, June 27-July 3, 1994.

Katharine Seelye   "Labor Dept. Agency Proposes Ban on All Smoking in the Workplace," *The New York Times*, March 26, 1994.

David Segal   "The Filtered Truth," *The Washington Monthly*, September 1993.

John Stamm   "Butting Heads over the Tobacco Tax," *Dollars & Sense*, June 1993.

Michael P. Traynor, Michael E. Begay, and Stanton A. Glantz   "New Tobacco Industry Strategy to Prevent Local Tobacco Control," *JAMA*, July 28, 1993.

Alexander Volokh   "Lighten Up," *UpDate*, July 1994. Available from the Competitive Enterprise Institute, 1001 Connecticut Ave. NW, Suite 1250, Washington, DC 20036.

Walter Williams   "Waxman Attacks Private Property," *Conservative Chronicle*, May 4, 1994.

Elizabeth M. Whelan   "Is Second-Hand Smoke *Really* a Threat to Our Health?" *Priorities*, Fall/Winter 1993.

Index